Aristonenes by Anne Kingsmill Finch

or, The Royal Shepherd.

A TRAGEDY

Anne Kingsmill was born in April 1661 (an exact date is not known) in Sydmonton, Hampshire.

Throughout her life Anne was involved in several Court cases that dragged on for years. These involved both a share of her parents estate for her education and later her and her husband's share of an inheritance.

In 1682, Anne became a maid of honour to Mary of Modena (wife of James, Duke of York, later King James II) at St James's Palace.

Anne's interest in poetry began at the palace, and she started writing her own verse. The Court however was no place for a woman to display any poetic efforts. Woman were not considered suitable for such literary pursuits.

At court, Anne met Colonel Heneage Finch. A courtier as well as a soldier. The couple married on 15th May 1684.

Index of Contents
DRAMATIS PERSONÆ
THE SCENES
ACT I
SCENE I
The SCENE changes to a Street in the Town of Phærea
The SCENE changed, discovers a Council-Chamber in Anaxander's Palace
ACT II
SCENE I
The SCENE changes to the Plains by the Woodside.
ACT III
SCENE I
The SCENE changes to the Plains.
ACT IV
SCENE I
ACT V
SCENE I
[The SCENE changes to a fine Tent.
ANNE KINGSMILL FINCH – A SHORT BIOGRAPHY
ANNE KINGSMILL FINCH – A CONCISE BIBLIOGRAPHY

DRAMATIS PERSONÆ

MEN
Aristomenes, Prince of the Messenians and Arcadians.

Aristor, Son to Aristomenes.
Alcander, A Principal Officer under Aristomenes.
Demagetus, Or the Royal Shepherd. Son to the Prince of Rhodes, under the Disguise of a Shepherd call'd Climander.
Arcasius, An old Lord, under the Habit of a Shepherd, Counsellor to Demagetus.
Anaxander, one of the Kings of Lacedemon (for they had always Two) and Leader of their Forces against Aristomenes.
Clarinthus, Chief Counsellor to Anaxander, a Lord of Sparta.
Clinias, A Shepherd keeping his Flock on the Plains of Messenia, close to the Walls of Phærea, with other Shepherds.

WOMEN

Herminia, Daughter to Aristomenes.
Barina, Her Woman and Confident.
Amalintha, Daughter to Anaxander.
Phila, Her Woman and Confident.
Thæta, and Lamia, Shepherdesses on the Plains of Messenia.
Soldiers, Officers, Guards, and Attendants, several Lords of the Spartan Council.

THE SCENES: Aristomenes's Camp near the Walls of Phærea; sometimes the Town of Phærea, and sometimes the Plains among the Shepherds.

ACT I

SCENE I

A pleasant Plain by a Wood-side; beyond it are seen, on one side, some of the Shepherds Hamlets; on the other (at a distance) the Walls of Phærea, a Garrison of the Lacedemonians.

Enter **CLIMANDER** meeting **ARCASIUS**; both drest like Shepherds.

CLIMANDER
Hast thou provided me a Horse and Arms,
A Sword, Arcasius, that when Time has freed me
From the Severe Injunctions of a Father,
May fill my Hand, instead of this vile Hook,
And fit it for the Work, a Prince is born to?

ARCASIUS
Unwillingly, I have obey'd your Orders;
But, 'till to-morrow's, and the next day's Sun
Shall light the angry, and contentious World,
Your Promise to your Father is in Force;
As well as the Assurance, which you gave,
That in my Custody these Arms shou'd rest,
Until that fatal Time demands their Use.

CLIMANDER

Call it not Fatal; Oh! that 'twere arriv'd!
That Aristomenes, the Spartan Terrour,
Were leading me, this moment, bravely on
Through Dangers, equal to the Cause he fights for,
Preserving these free Plains from foreign Bondage!
Though in the Strife this Body strew'd the Ground,
To Fame, and Publick Good an early Victim.

ARCASIUS

O wretched Rhodes! Thy Ruin is pronounc'd,
And thou beneath th'impending Plagues may'st perish;
Since He, whom Oracles appoint to Aid thee
Thus wishes with his Own, to sell thy Safety,
For the rash Praise of an intruding Warriour.

CLIMANDER

No more of Oracles!
Which oftner we fulfil by heedless Chance,
Than the vain Study to pursue their Meaning;
Which makes me banish, from my lab'ring Thoughts,
Those Mystick Words, which serve but to perplex them.

ARCASIUS

From Mine they will not part, nor shou'd from Yours;
Which to prevent, ev'n now I will repeat them;
The Isle of Rhodes shall be of Peace bereft,
Unless it by the Heir thereof be left,
And that He wed, ere he returns agen,
The Beauteous Daughter of the Best of Men;
Whose Father's presence there shall save the State,
And smooth the threatning Brow of angry Fate.

CLIMANDER

But, Who this Man, or, Where his Daughter is,
Was left in Darkness, to employ our Search:
Yet, in Obedience, Hither did I come
To feed a Flock, and mix with simple Swains;
Because the Priests, who sway in Princes Courts,
Declar'd, that perfect Innocence, and Virtue
Was to be found but in their lowly Rank,
And There, the Best of Men was to be sought for.

ARCASIUS

'Tis True, they did; and therefore urg'd our Prince;
That slighting (in a Case of such Importance)
The Pride of Titles, and of equal Birth,
You might espouse One of these Rural Maids,
Whose Parents harmless Presence in our Land
Might bring the Blessings of the Gods upon us;
And, lest the Wars (which still infest these Countries)

Shou'd tempt you from the Fates, and his Design,
How strictly did He Charge it on your Duty,
That, 'till the Time, which now, Two Days must end,
You shou'd not leave these Plains, to seek the Camp!

CLIMANDER
Nor have I done it, as Thyself can witness;
But here have spent the long and lazy Hours,
Carelessly stretch'd beneath some Sylvan Shade,
And only sent my Wishes to their Tents;
But ere the Battle (which is soon intended)
Shall meet in glorious Tryal of their Right,
I will be there, and side with the Messenians.

ARCASIUS
Oh! that you wou'd not!
That first your Native Country might be serv'd,
Think on her Danger, and your Sovereign's Will:
'Twas to the Reed, and not the wrangling Trumpet
He bid you listen, to secure his Peace;
Nor have you look'd with Love, as he requir'd,
On any Shepherdess, tho' ne'er so Fair,
Or born of Parents, harmless as their Flocks.
Low on my Knees, my Lord, let me prevail,

[He Kneels.

That, when the Time, decreed you, do's expire,
You will not prosecute this rash Design;
But go with me yet farther on these Plains,
And seek to please your Father, and the Gods,
In such safe, humble ways, as they direct us.

CLIMANDER
Nay, prithee, do not kneel; it grates my Nature:

[Raises him.

But trust me, when we have subdued these Countries
When Lacedemon's Kings shall sue for Peace,
And make great Aristomenes Returns
Agreeing to his Merits, and their Wrongs,
And I have gain'd such Honour as becomes me;
Whate'er thou doest request shall be observ'd:
And tho' my Soul finds such vast disproportion
Betwixt the Thoughts, with which she is inspir'd,
And those, that lodge in these poor Country Maids;
Yet shall my Duty o'er my Temper rise,
I'll trust (like Others) only to my Eyes,
And think, that Women in Perfection are,
Tho ne'er so Ignorant, if Young and Fair,

ARCASIUS
Ha!

[A Noise is heard of distant Drums.

Sure I hear the distant Sound of Drums. [Aside.
Heav'n grant what I've been told, and kept so secret,
Of a Design this Day to end the War,
Be not a Truth too tempting for my Reasons!

[Enter frighted, **THÆTA** and **LAMIA**, Shepherdesses.

LAMIA
Oh! may we here be safe, tell us Climander?
For all the Lawns, that lie beyond the Hill,
Where still our Flocks were us'd to feed in peace,
Are fill'd with War, and dark with flying Arrows:
The Sheep disperse, whilst none regard their Safety,
But call on Pan, to shield th' advent'rous Chief,
The noble Aristomenes from Danger.

CLIMANDER [Aside to **ARCASIUS**]
Hear me, Arcasius, hear and do not thwart me;
Not tye me to a few remaining Hours:
For, by the horrid Shield, that bears the Gorgon,
I Swear; if thou refuse to arm me now
With what I sent thee lately to provide,
These feet shall bear me sandal'd to the Battle,
This flow'ry Wreath shall mix with their stern Helmets,
And Death I'll take, if not impower'd to give it.

ARCASIUS
Oh! do not ask my Aid; but in this Tryal,
Call all your fainting Virtue to assist
And help you keep your Promise to your Father.

CLIMANDER
I did not promise him to be a Coward,
To let the Sound of War thus strike my Sense,
Yet keep my Heart in a cool, even Temper.
Hark! this way comes the Noise, and I will meet it.

[As he is going, a confus'd Noise and Cry is heard within.

ARCASIUS
They're Cries of Grief, and not the Shouts of Battle.
I hope All's past, lest He and Rhodes shou'd perish.

[Enter meeting, **CLIMANDER**, **CLINIAS**, and **OTHER SHEPHERDS**.

1st SHEPHERD
Ruin'd, Undone!

CLINIAS
Let every Shepherd weep!
Turn their sweet Harmony to Sighs and Groans!
To the fierce Wolves deliver up their Flocks,
And leave Messenia to the cruel Victor!

CLIMANDER
The Victor, Clinias! is the Fight then over?

CLINIAS
It is, and We again the Slaves of Sparta.

CLIMANDER
Then Aristomenes must sure be breathless,
And, if he's Dead, fall'n in his Country's Cause:
The Gods have giv'n Him Fame, whilst We are Wretched.

CLINIAS
Oh! He's not Dead, but Living in their Power,
Which, 'tis believ'd, they'll use with utmost Rigour:
Pressing too far on the Auxiliary Troops,
The Foe surrounding bore him from his Horse,
Then with the Thongs of their curs'd Cretan Bows
Bound his strong Arms, and lead him off, in Triumph.

CLIMANDER
Convert, ye Powers, to Blood and Tears that Triumph!
Rescue from their vile Hands the noble Prey,
And send him warmer Friends than Demagetus,   [Aside.
Who, knowing not his Person, lov'd his Valour!
O ill-tim'd Duty, how hast thou betray'd me!
Where is Aristor? Where's the brave Alcander?   [To them.

CLIMANDER
The first may share in his great Father's Fate,
For ought, as yet, the Army can discover:
Alcander heads, but cannot lead them on,
And 'tis believ'd they quickly will forsake him;
Such cold Dismay and Terrour has possess'd 'em!
Yet ere we part, forever part from hence,
(If so the cruel Tyrant shou'd Decree)
Let us appoint one sad and solemn Meeting,
Where all the Ensigns of our former Mirth
May be defac'd and offer'd to his Praise.
That made our Nights secure, and bless'd our Days.

1st SHEPHERD
So let it be!

Again, one Ev'ning on these Plains we'll meet.

2nd SHEPHERD
But never tread them more with chearful Feet.

[Exeunt **SHEPHERDS** and **SHEPHERDESSES**.

CLIMANDER
Cruel Arcasius! How hast thou undone me,
Charming me, with thy Tears, to this soft Circle,
Whilst the bright Spirit, Honour is gone by,
And borne away on never-turning Pinions!
Why wou'd'st thou thus contrive against my Fame,
And rob my fiery Youth of this first War,
(For which it languish'd with a Lover's Fondness)
By saying still 'twou'd last, 'till Time had freed me?
But I will yet pursue it thro' Despair,
And share their Ruin, tho' deny'd their Glory.

[As he's going **ARCASIUS** kneels.

ARCASIUS
Yet, this last time, behold my bended Knees,
Which if you slight shall of the Gods implore
A hasty Death, to fall on old Arcasius:
Nor think, this Posture means to cross your way;
For, by those Powers I swear; if they will Fight
As much, we hear 'tis doubted by the Shepherds,
I will not sue, to keep you from the Army,
Or bring on me your future Life's Reproaches.
Let me obtain but This, for all my Service,
To be first sent to sound their Disposition,
Which I'll relate with Truth, and help your Purpose:
In this Attempt Two Hours will not be lost;
Oh! give so much, to save his Life, that loves you.

CLIMANDER
Thou has obtain'd it, by thy promis'd Aid,
And my long Knowledge of the Truth that guides thee.
About It then, whilst, in that shady Grove,
I with impatience wait for thy Return.

ARCASIUS
Which shall not be prolong'd my Lord, believe me.

[Exeunt severally.

[Enter **SEVERAL SOLDIERS**, running over the Stage, and throwing away their Arms.

1st SOLDIER
Away, away, haste to the Woods for Shelter.

2nd SOLDIER
Do they begin to sally from the Town?

3rd SOLDIER
I know not; look behind him, he that will.
Here lies my Way—

[They run into the Wood.

[Enter more, doing as the former.

1st SOLDIER
Farewell the Wars! Oh! never such a General!

2nd SOLDIER
Never such Sorrow! never such a General!

[Enter more.

2nd SOLDIER
What, is the Army all dispers'd, and broken!   [To them.

3rd SOLDIER
No, but the Wisest of them do as We do.
Away, away—

[Enter **ALCANDER** meeting them.

ALCANDER
Why do ye fly my Friends, and cast these from ye?
For shame! like Men, that once have known their Use,
Take 'em again, and wait, or seek the Foe.

3rd SOLDIER
Seek 'em, for what?
We cannot find our General out amongst 'em:
'Tis thought they've made sure Work with him already;
And now you'd have us run upon their Swords.
We thank you, Captain. Come away, away!

[Exit follow'd by some **OTHERS**.

ALCANDER
Oh! yet my Fellow-Soldiers, stay and hear me;
Can ye so soon forget your Noble General,
Your Aristomenes, whose Courage fed ye,
And by whose Conduct, ye have slept securely
In reach of Foes, that trebled ye in Number!
Can ye forget the Care, that heal'd your Wounds;
The Tongue, that prais'd them; or those Liberal Hands,

That pour'd down Gold, faster than they your Blood!

1st SOLDIER
No; were he but amongst us, we'd Dye with him.

2nd SOLDIER
We are no Cowards, Captain, nor Ungrateful.
But since they say, He's Dead, What can we do?

ALCANDER
Go back, and keep a little while together;
At least, 'till there are Tydings from the Town:
Then, if he lives, we may attempt his rescue;
Or, if he's Dead, in a most just despair
Burn their accurst Phærea o'er their Heads,
And then disperse, when we're so far reveng'd.
Do this my Friends; Come, come, I know you will:
You lov'd the General—

1st SOLDIER
Cursed be He, that did not!

2nd SOLDIER
We will go back, but ne'er shall see him more.

3rd SOLDIER
Then we will Fight no more, that's sure enough.

4th SOLDIER
Howe'er, let's follow the brave Captain here,
And stay, 'till we're inform'd as he advises.

ALCANDER
Come, I will march before you.
Take up your Arms and trust, my Friends, to me:
Your Lives shall not be set on idle Hazards;
Lose no more time, but let us join the Army.

[They take up their Arms, and Exeunt.

[Enter **HERMINIA** and **BARINA**, Disguis'd like Shepherdesses.

HERMINIA
Alas! Barina, whither wilt thou lead me?

BARINA
To Safety, Madam, poor and humble Safety,
Which in those Hamlets, now within our Sight,
The Shepherds find, with whom we may partake it.

HERMINIA

Thus far indeed thou'st brought me on to seek it,
Urging the Danger of a Virgin's Honour,
When left defenceless to the Conqueror's Will:
But dost thou think, we may not thro' these Woods
Find out some gloomy Cave to Men unknown,
And there expiring, sleep secure for ever?

BARINA
Why shou'd we Dye,
Since Aristomenes may yet be Living?

HERMINIA
Oh! that thou hads't not named him!

[She starts and weeps.

'Till we were lodg'd, where Grief
Might have its Course; for now 'twill flow
And stop our farther Passage, barring the Sight
Which shou'd conduct our Steps.

BARINA
It must not Madam, nor must you indulge it,
But put on chearful Looks to suit this Habit,
And make the World believe you what you seem.

HERMINIA
I cannot do it.
In the midst of Sport
I shou'd forget the gay, fantastick Scene,
And drop these Tears, when Smiles were most expected.

BARINA
Then 'tis in vain farther to seek for Shelter:
Let us return and wait in your Pavilion,
'Till Anaxander shall command you thence
To serve the base Delight of some proud Spartan.

HERMINIA
Oh! yet avert that Fate, ye angry Powers!
I yield, Barina; make me what thou wilt:
See, I no more am sad; look on this Brow;
Canst thou read here that I have lost a Father,
The best, the fondest, and the dearest Father?
Forgive the tender Thought, that breeds this Change;
I'll weep it off, and smile again to please thee.

BARINA
No; I'll weep too, for his, that's past,
And your approaching Ruin.

HERMINIA
Alas! I had forgot, but now am Calm:
What must I do? indeed I will observe thee.

BARINA
Then not far hence, conceal'd within this Grove
Wait my Return, who must go find the Shepherds,
And frame some Story; that when you appear,
Thro' no Enquiries we become suspected:
And in my absence, be your Thoughts employ'd
To bend your Mind to what the Times require.

HERMINIA
To Fate and thy Advice I will submit,
Suit to my alter'd State my low Desire;
My Fare be plain, and homely my Attire,
My Tresses with a simple Fillet bind,
Face the hot Sun, and wither in the Wind;
In my parch'd Hand a rural Crook be found,
The Trees my Curtains, and my Bed the Ground:
That Fortune (who at Greatness aims her Blow)
When thus disguis'd may not a Princess know.

[Exeunt.

The **SCENE** changes to a Street in the Town of Phærea (the Lacedemonian Garrison) a **RABBLE** and many common **SOLDIERS** in the Street.

1st SOLDIER
All's done, all's done my Fellows.
We may now go home to our Wives, and our Shops.

1st RABBLE
Ay, that we may; we have caught him at last,
That has been our Back-friend so long,
As one may say–

2nd SOLDIER
Nay, I'll be sworn,
Thou never look'd'st him in the Face:
But we shall have the tossing, and the tumbling of him
As soon as ever the sowre-fac'd Senators
Have dismiss'd their Judgements upon him.

3rd RABBLE
Ay, I'll warrant ye, shall we;
Here, here he comes; bear back, bear back.

[**ARISTOMENES** bound and guarded is conducted over the Stage, the **RABBLE** crowding and following him with confus'd Cries and Shouts, Exeunt.

The **SCENE** changed, discovers a Council-Chamber in Anaxander's Palace: **ANAXANDER**, **CLARINTHUS**, and **SEVERAL LORDS OF SPARTA**.

ANAXANDER
Most, happily, my Lords, we now are met,
To see those Hands in servile Fetter's ty'd
Which broke the Bondage of the proud Messenians
Whom Sparta long had held in hard Subjection.
Ere yet their Captive General do's appear,
Be it amongst your selves, My Lords, resolved
What Course will answer best our Ends upon them.
Speak you, Clarinthus, for'most of the Assembly;
And then, let ev'ry one add what he pleases.

CLARINTHUS
Short be my Speech, and plain, as is the way
Which must secure what Lacedemon toils for:
Let him resign that Country, kept by him
From the entire Subjection, to our Yoke;
Or let his speedy Death deliver to Us
What his too active Life has long kept back.

ANAXANDER
What say the rest?—

ALL THE SENATE
All, all agree to this.

CLARINTHUS
No middle Course can be of use to Sparta.

A LORD
Bring in the Pris'ner; 'tis the King's Command.

[**ARISTOMENES** is brought in by the **GUARD**.

[**ARISTOR** in a Spartan Dress presses in amongst the **CROWD**, whilst **PHILA** appears at the Door.

ANAXANDER [To **CLARINTHUS**]
At last, we see the Hero can be Conquer'd,

CLARINTHUS
Not in his Looks; for they are haughty still,
And so his Mind will prove, if I mistake not.

ANAXANDER
That you, our Pris'ner now, of late our Foe,
Have urg'd that Country, where you rule in Chief,
To break our Yoke, and make Incursions on us,

Since known to all, will justify our Sentence
Which is; That you shall meet the Death deserv'd,
Unless to keep our Quiet for the future,
You bring again Messenia to our Sway,
Paying such Tribute, as shall be impos'd
By Us, the Lords of that offensive State.
This is the Choice, we kindly set before you,
And wish, that you wou'd take the safest Part,

ARISTOMENES
Enslave my Country, to secure my Life!
That Pow'r forbid it, under whose Protection
I've often fought her Battles with Success,
And drove th' ill-grounded War home to your Sparta!

CLARINTHUS
He braves us in his Bonds: then you wou'd Dye.

ARISTOMENES
I do not say I wou'd;
I am a Man, and Nature bars that saying:
Yet I dare Dye; no Spartan here, but knows it.
But since the Fates (whose Wills we best can read,
When thus unfolded in their dire Events)
Tell me by these vile Bonds I must submit;
Propose the gentlest Bargain you can make,
And if I find my Life bears equal Weight,
I am content to take it, else 'tis Yours.

ANAXANDER
'Tis not for Us to wave, or change our Terms,
Mistaken Man, who think not of our Power,
And that we may command what we propose:
Since the first Sally, now, must take Possession
Of what your frighted Rout will soon abandon.

ARISTOMENES
My frighted Rout!
Ye basely wrong with foul reproachful Names
Those valiant Troops, which yet ye cannot Conquer:
For know, thou proud insulting Anaxander,
There's at their head a resolute young Man,
That will not 'bate thee in his strict Account
One Sigh or Groan, thy Tortures or thy Dungeons
Shall wrest in Dying from his Father's Bosom.

[**ANAXANDER** and the **SENATE** talk among themselves, whilst **ARISTOR** comes forward upon the Stage.

But there he stands! [Aside seeing **ARISTOR**.
Aristor thro' that Spartan Dress I view,

And ne'er, till now, wish'd not to see my Son.
Protect him from their Knowledge, some kind Pow'r,
If Youth, or Virtue e'er engag'd your Pity!

CLARINTHUS
Let it be so, and speedily perform'd,
[Aloud.
For He'll ne'er yield to what has been demanded.

ANAXANDER
You nam'd the Dungeon, with a Threaten too
Of swift Revenge, thinking to fright our Justice:
But we'll take care, first, to perform our Part,
Then, venture what your daring Son can offer.
The Dungeon is his Sentence, thither bear him.

ARISTOR
Not till this Hand has done a swifter Justice.

[Draws and runs at **ANAXANDER**.

ANAXANDER
Ha! what means this, my Guards!

[He avoids the thrust: **PHILA** runs in.

PHILA
Help, Soldiers, help; seize that distracted Spartan.
Who now has got a Sword; Disarm, and take him.

[They disarm him.

ARISTOR
'Tis false; stand off, ye Slaves, and know I am—

PHILA
Oh! stop his Mouth; for if he raves, he Dyes.

[They stop his Mouth with a Handkerchief.

ARISTOMENES
As sure as now he Lives, had he spoke more   [Aside.
Therefore be blest the Stratagem that stopt him!

ANAXANDER
What means this, Phila; speak, Who is this Madman?

PHILA
One by a Friend entrusted to my Care,
Sent from the Country here to find a Cure;
But hearing, as the Croud pass'd by his Lodgings,

That Aristomenes wou'd soon be Sentenc'd,
He broke his Ward, and fancy'd He must save him.
I have pursu'd him, 'till I am faint with Crying,
And am confounded at his frantick Passion.
Oh! Royal Sir, forgive it–

ANAXANDER
We do, and pity him: remove him hence,
Then, to thy Mistress, my dear Daughter, Go
And say we now again shall soon see Sparta.

PHILA
I shall my Lord!
[To the **GUARDS**.
Now follow me, I'll lead ye to his Lodgings.

[Exit **PHILA** with the **GUARDS** bearing off **ARISTOR**

ARISTOMENES
Whoe'er she be,
May Heaven reward her, if she means his Safety. [Aside.
Now I can meditate on my own Fortunes,
And slight the worst can reach me.

ANAXANDER
He's deep in Thought which may produce a Change.
Again, I'll try him –
[To **CLARINTHUS**
Now, Aristomenes, that this wild Chance
Has given you time to think upon our Sentence,
Have you enough consider'd of its Horror,
To bend your stubborn Will to our Demands?

ARISTOMENES
Yes, Anaxander, I have weigh'd it well:
That active Faculty, which we call Phancy,
Soon as you spoke, dragg'd me thus bound by Slaves
Thro' the throng'd Streets, exciting several Passions;
The Barb'rous Croud shouted their clamorous Joy,
Because unpunish'd they might sport with Blood;
Old Men and Matrons, destin'd long for Death,
With envious Pleasure saw me forc'd before them
To tread that Path, in spight of vigorous Nature,
Whilst tender Virgins turned aside their Heads,
And dropt, in Silence, the soft Tears of Pity:
But, Oh! the Soldiers; from the Soldier's hands
Methoughts I saw their Swords neglected thrown,
When Fortune shew'd they cou'd not save the Bravest
(If once she frown'd) from such a Fate as mine.

CLARINTHUS

He'll move the Croud; urge him to speak directly.

ANAXANDER
All this is from the purpose; plainly tell
Whether you'll meet our Mercy, or the Dungeon.

ARISTOMENES
My Train of Thoughts to that dark Cave had led me;
I stood reclined upon the horrid Brim,
And gaz'd into it, 'till my baffl'd Sight
Piercing beyond the many jetting Rocks
That help to break by turns the falling Body,
Was lost in Shades, where it must rest for-ever:
And ready now to be pushed rudely off,
This was my last, and best Reflection on it,
That there dwelt Peace, which is not to be found
In his dark Bosom, that has sold his Country.

ANAXANDER
Away with him to instant Tryal of it:
See this obey'd, and plunge him headlong down;
There, he'll have Time, if Life, for such fine Thoughts.
Away, and bring me word it is perform'd.

[Exeunt **ANAXANDER** and **LORDS**.

[**ARISTOMENES** born off.

[**RABBLE** and **SOLDIERS**
Away, away; the Dungeon, the Dungeon.
Peace and Prosperity to Lacedemon!

[Exeunt.

ACT II

SCENE I

A Room in the Palace. **ARISTOR** alone.

ARISTOR
I've torn with Cries the Roof of this vile Mansion.
And from that Window, barr'd too closely up
To give me leave to leap upon their Heads,
Have curs'd the Croud, and told 'em whose I am:
At which they laugh, and cry, 'tis Phila's Madman.

[He attempts but cannot force the Door.

Confusion! that she dares confine me thus!

Whilst my free Thoughts, unfollow'd by my Hand,
Must see that cursed Deed, they can't prevent.
Oh! Aristomenes, my noble Father!
Hear me, ye Fates, and let me but Revenge him;
Give me Revenge; and now, methinks, I grasp it,
Broke thro' his Guards, I seize upon the Tyrant,
And stab him thus, and thus –
[He acts all this.
Then bear him to the Ground, thus falling on him,
And to his Heart thus tearing my wide way.
Oh! O', O', O',–

[Throws himself upon the Ground.

[Enter **AMALINTHA**, the Door by one without immediately lock'd after her.

AMALINTHA
Where is this wretched Mourner?
Oh! let me find him, tho' to raise his Sorrows
With the sad Sound of my repeated Groans.
Ha! on the Ground! then be it too my Seat!

[Sits on the Ground by him.

For I will share in this Excess of Grief,
As well as in the Days of milder Fortune,
I bore a part in Love, that knew no Measure.
O Aristomenes! oh! my Aristor!

[She puts her Handkerchief before her Eyes weeping.

ARISTOR
Whoe'er thou art, repeat again that Sound:
Such groans shall hourly issue from his Dungeon,
And fright the bloody Spartans into Madness.

[He looks up.

Ha! sure I shou'd know that Form, that Shape, those Limbs,
That lab'ring Bosom, and those Locks dishevel'd:
But take not from thy Face that friendly Cloud;
Do not expose it, lest thro' all its Charms
My deep Revenge find out whose Stamp it bears,
And urge me on to something Dark and Fatal.

AMALINTHA
This from Aristor! this to Amalintha!

[She rises and shews her face.

ARISTOR

Why wou'd'st thou tempt me thus advent'rous Maid,
And bring the blood of Anaxander near me?

[Coming up fiercely to her.

Canst thou too fondly think, that Love's soft Bands,
His gentle Cords of Hyacinths and Roses,
Wove in the dewy Spring, when Storms are silent,
Can tye these Hands, provok'd by horrid Murther!
Oh! do not trust it—
But fly this Ground, while I have Power to bid thee.

AMALINTHA
Aristor, no; my Flight shall not preserve me:
The Life, I've kept but to indulge your Love,
Now to this loud, mistaken Rage I offer.
Take it, Oh! take it; Means cannot be wanting,
Altho' no Instrument of Death be near you:
This Hair, these flatter'd Locks, these once-lov'd Tresses
Round my sad Neck thus knit will soon perform it;
Or, on these trembling Lips your Hand but prest
Will send the rising Breath down to my Heart,
And break it, telling who deny'd it Passage.

ARISTOR
Tryal beyond the Strength of Man and Lover!

AMALINTHA
Or, if you wou'd be quicker in Dispatch,
Speak but a few such Words, as now you utter'd,
And my poor hov'ring Soul will fly before 'em.
Farewel Aristor, see! the Work is done:
I did but think I heard their killing Sound,
And the bare Fancy saves you farther Study.

[She faints, he catches her in his Arms.

ARISTOR
Oh! stop the glorious Fugitive a moment;
And I will whisper to it such Repentance,
Such Love, such Fondness, such unheard-of Passion,
As shall confine it to it's beauteous Mansion.
Thus let me hug, and press thee into Life,
And lend thee Motion from my beating Heart,
To set again the Springs of thine in working.

AMALINTHA
I hear your Summons, and my Life returns:
But tell me, ere again so firm 'tis fixt
That it must cost an Agony like this,
To let it out to Liberty and Ease,

Will you not hate me for my Father's Guilt?

ARISTOR
By the soft Fires of Love, that fill my Breast,
And dart through all the Horrors of my Soul,
Like Heaven's bright Flashes in a Night of Shadows,
I will not hate, or e'er reproach thee more:
Yet let me breathe so gently one Complaint,
So gently, that it may not break thy Peace,
Tho' it for ever has discarded mine,
And ask, why you thus cruelly wou'd use me,
Why, have me seiz'd, and bound with frantick Fetters,
Snatch'd from my Duty by a Woman's wile,
And here confin'd, whilst my great Father perish'd?

AMALINTHA
'Twas none of mine, by your dear self I swear;
It was the Fates design and Phila's action;
She saw you thus disguis'd amongst the Croud,
And, ere she would acquaint me with your Danger,
Follow'd to watch the means how to prevent it.

ARISTOR
I will belief you to my Heart's relief,
Which must have broke, had your Consent been with her.
But, Amalintha, now my Rage is gone,
And Love thro' this mistake has forc'd his way,
It spreads before my Thoughts the gaudy Scene
Of those Delights, which have been once allow'd it;
Brings to my Phancy in their softest Dress
The gentle Hours, that told our private Meetings;
Shews me the Grove, where, by the Moon's pale Light
We've breath'd out tender Sighs, 'till coming Day
Has drawn them deeper, warning us to part,
Which ne'er we did, 'till some new Time was set
For the return of those transporting Pleasures.

AMALINTHA
And so again, Aristor, we'll contrive,
And so again, we'll meet, and sigh, and love.

ARISTOR
Oh! O', O', – Amalintha!

AMALINTHA
Oh! why that Groan, that deep, that deathlike Groan!

ARISTOR
When Soul and Body part, it can't be softer;
And I must leave thee, Soul to sad Aristor.
With all those Pleasures which I but repeated,

As dying Friends will catch one last Embrace
Of what they know, they must forego forever.

AMALINTHA
Indeed, you've call'd my wand'ring Fancy back
From those Delights, where 'twou'd have endless stray'd:
But, my Aristor! (for I'll call you mine,
Though all the Stars combine against my Title,
And bar fulfilling of the Vows they've witness'd)
Tell me, tho' we must ne'er in Nuptials join,
May we not meet, and at this distance sigh?
And when I've hoarded up a Stock of Tears,
Which in the Spartan's sight I dare not lavish,
Oh! tell me, if I may not seek you out,
And in large Showers thus pour them down before you?

[She weeps.

ARISTOR
Cease to oppress me more; thou weeping Beauty,
And think with what vast Storms my Soul is toss'd!

[Comes up to hear earnestly.

Think too, that but to gaze upon thee thus,
To stand in reach of thy Ambrosial Breath,
And hear thy Voice, sweet as the Ev'ning Notes,
When in still Shades the Shepherds sooth their Loves,
I wou'd not mind an Army in my way,
Or stop at raging Seas, or brazen Towers.
Yet, Amalintha, tho' I Dye to speak it,
Yet we must part, we must, my Amalintha!

AMALINTHA
Never to meet agen? Tell me but that.

ARISTOR
Alas! not I, the Fates can only tell it:
Let them make even one Account betwixt us,
And give this Hand the Liberty to seal it.
And we'll in spight of vengeful Thunder join,
If then, thy Heart be as resolv'd as mine.

AMALINTHA
No: on those Terms you mean, we must not meet:
But since those Fates deny it to your Power,
The Will I to your mighty Wrongs forgive,

[From without the door.

PHILA

Madam, you'll be surpriz'd; haste to return:
Your Father's now just going to your Lodgings.

ARISTOR
All Plagues and Curses meet him!

[Aside.

AMALINTHA
Oh! then I must be gone.
A little time will call the State to Council;
And when the Croud by that is thither drawn,
One I will send to wait on your Escape:
And if you tempt new Dangers, know Aristor
That Amalintha too will perish in them.

ARISTOR
Fear not, my Love.

PHILA [From without]
Haste, Madam, haste, or we are all Undone.

AMALINTHA
So from his few short Moments calls away
A gasping Wretch, the cruel BIrd of Prey;
Bids him make haste th' Eternal Shades to find,
And leave like me, all that is Dear behind.

ARISTOR
Whilst, like the Friend that's sadly weeping by,
I see the much lov'd Spirit from me fly;
And with vain Cries pursue it to that Coast,
Where it must land, and my weak Hopes be lost.

[He leads her to the Door, and returns speaking as he's going out at the Other.

Now, let Revenge awhile sustain my Heart,
And Fate yet close my Life with some exalted part!

[Exit.

The Stage darken'd represents the Inside of a Dungeon, **ARISTOMENES** lying down in it, and struggling as coming out of a Swoon.

ARISTOMENES
At last 'tis vanquish'd; and my soaring Spirits
Dispel the gloomy Vapours, that oppress'd them,
And cloath'd my Dreams with more than mortal Horrour.
So low in my deep Phancy was I plung'd,
That o'er my Head impetuous Rivers rush'd,
And Mountains grew betwixt our World and me:

Hungry and Cold, methought I wander'd on
Thro' fruitless Plains, that Food nor Comfort nourish'd,
'Till hideous Serpents twisted me about,
And drew me to their Den all foul and loathsome;
But I will quit the Bed, that breeds such Visions,
And summon all my Officers to Council;
For with to-morrow's Dawn we'll storm Phærea.

[He walks about feeling for the Door.

Ha! where's the Door, my Tent is sure transform'd,
And all I touch is Rock that streams with Dew.
Oh! that I'd slept, that I had slept for ever!

[He starts.

Yes, Anaxander, yes! thou worst of Furies!
I know thy Dungeon now, and my dark Ruin:
Yet why, ye Fates, since fall'n below your Succour,
Wou'd ye thus cruelly restore my Senses,
To make me count my Woes by tedious Moments,
Dye o'er again, choak'd by unwholsome Damps,
Parch'd up with Thirst, or clung with pining Hunger,
Borne piecemeal to the Holes of lurking Adders,
Or mould'ring to this Earth, where thus I cast me?

[Throws himself on the Ground.

Musick is heard without the **SCENE**, after it has play'd awhile and ceases, He speaks.

How, Harmony! nay then the Fiends deride me:
For who, but they, can strike Earth's sounding Entrails,
Or with low Winds thus fill her tuneful Pores?
Oh! that some Words of horrid Sense wou'd join it,
To tell me where I might conclude my Sorrows!

1st VOICE
Fallen Wretch! make haste, and Dye!
To that last Asylum fly,
Where no anxious Drops of Care,
Where no sighing Sorrows are,
Friends or Fortune none deplore,
None are Rich, and none are Poor,
Nor can Fate oppress them more.
To this last Asylum fly,
Fallen Wretch! make haste and Dye!

[The **VOICE** ceases.

ARISTOMENES
Thou counsell'st rightly; show me but the way,

And with the Speed thou urgest I'll obey thee.

[He rises.

The **VOICE** Sings again.

1st VOICE
A pointed Rock with little pains
Will split the Circle of thy Brains,
To thy Freedom I persuade thee,
To a wat'ry Pit will lead thee,
Which has no glorious Sun-beam seen,
No Footstep known, or bord'ring Green,
For thousand rolling Ages past.
Fallen Wretch! to this make haste,
To this last Asylum fly.
Fallen Wretch! make haste and Dye!

ARISTOMENES
I come, thou kind Provoker of Despair,
Which still is nearest Cure, when at the Highest.
I come, I come–

[Going towards the **VOICE**, another Sings at the other side, upon which He stops and listens.

2nd VOICE
Stay, oh! stay; 'tis all Delusion,
And wou'd breed thee more Confusion.
I, thy better Genius, move thee,
I, that guard, and I, that love thee;
I, who in thy rocky way,
Cloth'd in Eagles Feathers lay,
And in safety brought thee down,
Where none living e'er was known.
Chearful Hope I bring thee now,
Chearful Hope the Gods allow,
Mortal, on their Pleasures wait,
Nor rush into the arms of Fate.

[The **VOICE** ceases.

ARISTOMENES
To hope, is still the Temper of the Brave:
And tho' a just Despair had dispossess'd it,
Yet, thus encourag'd, will I trust the Gods
With those few Moments, Nature has to spare me;
Nor follow thee, thou bad persuading Spirit.
Yet tell me, who thou art, and why thou tempt'st me?

1st VOICE
I thy evil Genius am,

To Phærea with thee came;
Hung o'er thee in the murd'ring Croud,
And clapp'd my dusky Wings aloud;
Now endeavour'd to deceive thee,
And will never, never, leave thee.

2nd VOICE
I'll protect him from thy Pow'r.

1st VOICE
I shall find a careless Hour.

2nd VOICE
Laurels He again shall wear,
War and Honour's Trumpet hear.

1st VOICE
For one fatal, famous Day,
He his dearest Blood shall pay.
Hear it ye repeating Stones,
And confirm it by your Groans!

[A dismal Groan is heard round the Dungeon.

ARISTOMENES
What all this Bellowing for a Conqueror's Death!
The Field of Honour is his Bed of Ease;
He toils for't all the Day of his hard Life,
And lays him there at Night, renown'd and happy:
Therefore his Threat was vain malicious Fury.

1st VOICE
Now away, away I fly;
For hated Good is rushing by.

[Here the **VOICE** ceases quite.

A Machine, like a **FOX**, runs about the Dungeon smelling, and rushes against **ARISTOMENES**, who taking it for his evil Genius, catches at it, and speaks.

ARISTOMENES
What! hast thou Substance too, and dar'st assault me!
Nay then, thou shalt not 'scape; I'll seize and grapple with thee,
And by my conqu'ring Arm o'ercome thy Influence.
Fool that I was! to think, it cou'd be vanquisht.
This is some rav'ning Beast; the Fur betrays it;
A Fox, I think, teach me to be as subtle,
Extremity, thou Mother of Invention!

[He catches it.

I have it now; and where it leads, will follow.
My better Genius do's this Hour preside:
Be strong that Influence, and thou my Guide.

[Exit, led out by the **FOX**.

The **SCENE** changes to the Plains by the Woodside.

[Enter from the Wood **HERMINIA** alone and faint.

HERMINIA
Here 'twas she left me; but so far I've stray'd,
Unheeding every thing, but my sad Thoughts,
That my faint Limbs no longer can support me.
Oh! let me rest; and if 'tis Death I feel,
A Guest more welcome none yet entertain'd.

[She sits down, leaning against a Tree.

[Enter **CLIMANDER** looking towards the Camp, as expecting the returns of **ARCASIUS**.

CLIMANDER
He has exceeded much the time prefixt;
And yet, I wou'd not doubt him:
I've climb'd the Hill, better to view the Camp;
And all are fixt, and motionless as Death.
Therefore awhile I will command my Patience:
He cannot now be long –

[He turns and sees **HERMINIA** and gazes earnestly on her.

–Ha! Who lies there?
A lovely Shepherdess; but faint she seems.
Say, beauteous Maid, if so much Strength is left,
How best a Stranger, may assist, or serve you!

[He kneels down by her.

She do's not speak; but looks into my Heart,
And melts it to the softness of her Eyes.
Hard by, a Spring clear as the Tears she drops,
Runs bubbling under a delicious Shade:
Water, thence fetch'd in a Pomegranate's rind,
May call her fainting Spirits to their office.

[He goes out.

HERMINIA
He's gone, but quickly will return again;
Yet he's so gentle sure I need not fear him:

Tho' at his first approach my Heart beat high,
'Till Halcyon sounds, and words of Pity calm'd it;
Nay, something courtly in them was imply'd:
And if the Swains are polish'd, all like him,
Their humble Sheds may scorn our ruder Greatness.

[Enter again **CLIMANDER** with Water in a Pomegranate-Shell.

CLIMANDER
Pan! if thou e'er did'st hear a Shepherd's Prayer,
Endue this Water, sacred to thy Name,
With all the Vertues, needful to restore her.

[She drinks.

HERMINIA
Your Pray'r is heard; kind Shepherd take my Thanks,
And He, whom you invok'd, reward you largely!

CLIMANDER
Oh! You may far outdo all He can grant,
In but declaring where you feed your Flocks,
And to what Shade, when Phoebus hottest shines,
You lead those happy Sheep, to 'scape his Fury;
That I, exposing mine to the wide Plains,
May seek you out, and sigh till Night before you.

HERMINIA
Alas! I have no Flocks, or Skill to guide them;
No leafy Hamlet, strew'd with painted Flowers;
Or mossy Pillow, to repose my Head:
But wander from a distant, fatal Place,
Where I have lost my Parents, and my Succour,
And now, in such a Habit as becomes it,
Seek the low Plains, to learn the Art you practice.

CLIMANDER
She may be Noble then; and for her Form,
'Tis sure the fairest that my Eyes e'er fix'd on.   [Aside.
Who were your Parents, gentle Maid, declare?

HERMINIA
They were not mean, and yet I must conceal them:
My Mother early Dy'd; but Fame has told me,
She'd all Perfections, which make Others Proud,
Yet wore them, as she knew not they adorn'd her.
And be, in this, my Father's Praise exprest:
That by an Oracle He was confest
Of all the Græcian Race to be the Best.

CLIMANDER

The Best of Men! and you the Fairest Woman!
And in a Moment I the greatest Lover!

[He speaks this transportedly and seizes her Hand, which he kisses.

Whilst to complete my Bliss, by Heav'ns decree
These Beauties all are mine, and thus I claim them.

HERMINIA
Protect me all ye Powers, that wait on Virtue,
From the dark Ends of such unruly Transports!

[She takes her Hand away hastily and rises.

Nor dare, presumptuous Swain, once to renew them,
Or tempt more Dangers than a Crook can answer!

CLIMANDER
A Man there lives not, shou'd have urg'd that to me,
Built round with Steel, or plung'd all o'er in Styx.
Then, let your Beauty's Triumphs be complete,
Which, after such a Threat, can bend my Knee,
And make me sue for Pardon, as for Life.

HERMINIA
I can forgive, whilst I forbid such Language;
Since She, who yields to have her Beauty worshipp'd,
Must pay too much to him, that brings the Incense.

CLIMANDER
To Me, you cannot, 'tis a Debt to Fate.
Your Heart is mine; the amorous Stars ordain it,
Which smiling, hung o'er my auspicious Birth,
And not an angry Planet cross'd their Influence:
They bid me Love, and the Harmonious God
When askt, what Path shou'd lead me on to Glory,
Sent forth a Sound, that charm'd the hoary Priest,
And said, a Passion, soft as that, must bless me.
Then, do not strive to disappoint their Purpose,
Or quench Celestial Flames with Scorn or Coldness.
Oh! that a Smile might tell me, that you wou'd not,
A gentle Word, a Look, a Sigh confirm it,
Or any sign, that bears the stamp of Love!
But 'tis in vain, and some more happy Youth
Has drawn my Lot, and mock'd foretelling Phoebus.

HERMINIA
I must not leave you with a Thought that wrongs me:
For know, no Passion e'er possess'd this Breast,
Nor will the mighty Griefs, that now have seiz'd it,
E'er yield to give a softer Guest admittance.

But my Companion comes; Shepherd farewell!
When next we meet, if Heav'n that Moment sends,
For your Assistance lent, we may be Friends.

CLIMANDER
Heav'n can't be true, if it no more affords,
Nor Oracles explain themselves by Words.
Let talking Age the Joys of Friendship prove,
Beauty for Youth was made, and Youth alone for Love.

[Exeunt severally.

ACT III

SCENE I

A Myrtle-Grove with a Fountain belonging to Anaxander's Palace.

Enter **AMALINTHA** and **PHILA**

AMALINTHA
Why had not I a bar'brous Spartan Soul,
Unapt for Love, and harsh, as our rude Customs!
Or why, ye cruel Fates! did you deny
My Birth to be among the neighb'ring Swains,
Where, on the flow'ry Banks of smooth Panisus
I might have sat, and heard the gentle Vows
Of some protesting Shepherd, uncontroul'd!

PHILA
'Twas on those fatal Plains, I well remember,
That first your Eyes encounter'd with Aristor's.

AMALINTHA
Yes, in a Chace we met, when Truce allow'd it,
Where the young Prince, whom I too much had mark'd
Thro' all the graceful Toils of that blest Day,
Redeem'd my Life, with Hazard of his own,
From the chas'd Boar, that now had almost seiz'd me.

PHILA
When I arriv'd the first of all your Train,
I heard you thank him for the gen'rous Rescue.

AMALINTHA
I did; yes Phila, with my Heart I thank'd him,
And laid it down a Ransom for my Life:
Since when, how often in this Place we've met,
And with what Pleasure, thou alone can'st tell,

The only Friend, and witness of our Passion.
But, prithee go, and keep off all Intruders,

[Exit **PHILA**.

Whilst with my Sorrows now I tread this Grove,
Which shou'd not thrive, when all our Hopes are blasted.

[She walks into the Grove.

From the other Door, the **FOX** runs over the Stage, follow'd soon after by **ARISTOMENES**, his Hands foul with Earth.

ARISTOMENES
Farewell my wild Companion, and my Leader!

[Pointing to the **FOX**.

Henceforth thy Figure, in my Ensigns borne,
Shall tell the World (if e'er I 'scape these Walls)
That 'twas thy Conduct drew me from my Bondage.
How fair this Grove appears to my loath'd Dungeon!

[He sees the Fountain.

Oh! welcome to my Sight, thou gentle Spring!
Ne'er did'st thou cool a Thirst, that rag'd like mine:
I bow my Knees upon thy mossy Brim,

[He kneels and lays his Mouth to the Stream.

And as they drank, ere Art had worsted Nature,
Draw thy refreshing Stream to my scorch'd Entrails.

[Drinks again.

Again, O Nectar, most delicious!
This favour more, and then I quit thy Borders.

[Washes the Earth off his Hands, and rises.

[Re-enter **AMALINTHA**.

AMALINTHA
Oh! 'tis all dismal, now that Love is absent,
Faded the Flow'rs, and with'ring ev'ry Branch:
Whilst thro' the Leaves the sad, and sighing Winds,
Methinks, all say, the Hours of Bliss are past;
And here, we ne'er shall meet each other more.

[**ARISTOMENES** comes towards her.

Ha! What Intruder do my Eyes behold?
A Stranger, and invade my private Walks,
The Doors too all secur'd! Tell me how you came.

ARISTOMENES
As comes the Mole, by painful working upwards,
Till the sweet Air beat on my clammy Brows.

AMALINTHA
There's something mystical in what you utter;
Which (tho' offended with your Presence here)
I wou'd be glad farther to have Unriddl'd.

[Draws her Dagger.

This be my Guard; and now you may proceed,
And, if you dare, discover who you are.

ARISTOMENES
I'd not deny my Name, to 'scape that Dungeon,

[Pointing behind the Scenes.

From whence these Hands have dug my way to Light.
'Tis Aristomenes that stands before you.

AMALINTHA
O blest and strange Surprise!   [Aside.

ARISTOMENES
Now, if you have a Soul for noble Deeds,
As 'tis reported of you Spartan Ladies,
By my Escape your Fame shall rise so high,
That ne'er an ancient Heroes shall outsoar it:
If not, I know the Place from whence I came,
And 'twill be told with more uncommon Things,
Which shall make up the Story of my Fortunes,
That I alone liv'd to be there twice Bury'd.

[She looks about.

Nay, look not round; for if you fear you wrong me,
I wou'd not injure you, to gain my Safety.

AMALINTHA
Nor wou'd I fail to help you to secure it,
For all that Lacedemon holds most Precious.
I gaz'd about, lest any were in sight,
That might prevent my dear Design to save you.
Support me, as I walk, like one that serv'd me,

And when they have unlock'd that Postern-door,
I'll give you some Command before the Guard,
Which to perform they shall admit your Passage:
Or this must force it, if your evil Stars

[Gives him her Dagger.

Have plac'd such there, as know and wou'd detain you.

ARISTOMENES
As long as Life, I'll proudly wear this Favour.

AMALINTHA
 Oh! haste, my Lord, lose not this precious moment.

ARISTOMENES
No, stay; and ere I take one step tow'rds Freedom,
Let me be told, to whose blest Aid I owe it;
And how I may discharge so vast a Debt:
Tho' I, and all that's dear to me shou'd perish,
I wou'd not stir, 'till satisfy'd in this.

AMALINTHA
Know then, my Lord—
Tho' whilst I speak, I tremble for your Danger,
That to declare my Name, might work my Ruin:
But since such Gratitude crowns your great Virtues,
I have a Blessing to implore from you,
When the full Time shall ripen and reveal it;
Harder, I fear, to grant, and much more dear
Than what I now assist you to preserve.

ARISTOMENES
By Liberty, which none like me can value,
By new-recovered Light, and what it shews me,
Your brighter Form, with yet a fairer Mind,
By all the ties of Honour, here I swear;
Be that untouch'd, and your Request is granted.

AMALINTHA
Of you, my Lord, and of the list'ning Gods
I ask no more—but, that you haste to 'scape:
Without that Gate the open Champain lies.
May Fortune, which the hardest Part has done,
Crown her great Work, and lead you safely on!

[Exit **ARISTOMENES** leading her.

[Enter **PHILA** weeping.

PHILA

What shall I say, or how reveal this to her?
Is't now enough, ye Gods, we bear our own,
That thus you suffer the vain trifler Love
To bring the Griefs of others too upon us!

[**AMALINTHA** returns.

AMALINTHA
Oh! Phila, I such Tydings have to tell thee,
But thou hast chill'd them in a Moments space
With that cold dew that trickles from thine Eyes.
Is not Aristor safe?–
Thou say'st he is not, in that weeping silence:
But lives he yet? if this thou do'st not answer,
My Death shall free thee from all farther Questions.

PHILA
Yet he do's live:
But oh! that some free Tongue, that lov'd you less,
Cou'd tell how little time that Life must last
To you so precious, and I fear so fatal!

AMALINTHA
Go on: and if thou kill'st me with the Story,
Believe thou'st crown'd the Kindness of thy Life,
By giving endless Rest to her that wants it.

PHILA [Weeping]
I cannot speak–

AMALINTHA
Then one, that can, I instantly must seek for.

[Going out.

PHILA
Publick Enquiry pulls his Ruin on her.
Stay, Madam, stay, and since it must be told,
Know that Aristor, soon as free to do it,
Again into your Father's presence rush'd,
And makes a new attempt upon his Person,
But missed his Blow, was seiz'd, and in Confinement
Now waits but the assembling of the Council,
Throughly to be examin'd, and discover'd.

AMALINTHA
Darkness, and Night surround me.
With this Relief to my sad Bed I go,

[Siezes **PHILA'S** dagger.

There wrapt in horrid Shades will lay me down,
And, when thou com'st charg'd with the heavy News,
Beware, no tedious Circumstance detail,
No fruitless Pray'r, or word of Comfort 'scape thee;
But with a Voice, such as the Dying use,
Bid me expire—
—Then to my Father go,
And say, he kill'd his Daughter in his Foe;
Who knowing, she his Temper cou'd not move,
Th' excess of Hate paid with th' excess of Love.

[Exit weeping and leaning on **PHILA**.

The **SCENE** changes to the Plains.

[Enter **CLIMANDER**.

CLIMANDER
All Patience this wou'd tire—
I will not wait the Trifler's slow return,
But go my self (tho' thus unarm'd) amongst them.

[He is going and meets **ARCASIUS**.

Art thou at length come back!
If 'twou'd not waste more time to blame thy stay,
Old loit'ring Man! I shou'd reprove thee for it.

ARCASIUS
'Twas vain to move, 'till I had seen the utmost.

CLIMANDER
The utmost! What was that, will they not Fight?
Not Dye for such a General!

ARCASIUS
My Lord, they will not—
Tho' brave Alcander tries to urge their Fury,
And wastes his own, to put new Life into them:
Sometimes he weeps, and throws his Helmet from him,
Kneels to his Troops, and wooes them to Compassion,
Which draws a gen'ral sympathizing Show'r,
And makes him think, he has obtain'd his Purpose:
Then on his fiery Steed in haste he leaps,
And cries, Come on; but not an Ensign waves,
Or any Motion seconds the Design.
The Meaner sort cry out for aloud for Pay,
And mutiny to be discharg'd the Service.

CLIMANDER

Base, mercenary Slaves! Yet these I'll use:
The Gold and Jewels which my Father gave,
Will fire their Souls, insensible of Duty;
And by it's aid, I'll gain what most I thirst for.
A King his Claim but to one Kingdom lays,
Wide as the Universe is boundless Praise.
This shining Mass shall buy a glorious Name,
They purchase all the World, who purchase Fame.

[He is going.

ARCASIUS
Since you're determin'd to attempt these Dangers,
Let me declare the Time to be expir'd,
Which bound you in your Promise to your Father:
By Artifice I wrought you to believe
Those Days remain'd, which are indeed run out.
Your Soul may now be free, and Heaven protect you!

CLIMANDER
For this discov'ry I'll return another
Worthy thy knowledge, when we meet again:
But now make haste, and from its deep concealment,
In the low Earth, fetch me the Wealth I mention'd.
About these Woods thy quick Return shall find me.

[Exeunt.

[Enter **HERMINIA** and **BARINA**.

BARINA
See we are come to soon; I said 'twou'd prove so.

HERMINIA
It is no matter, long we shall not wait.

[**BARINA** looks out for the **SHEPHERDS**.

I dare not tell her, that I like this Shepherd,
Nor yet indeed scarce own it to my self.
'Tis strange, my Mind shou'd sink thus with my Fortunes;
Yet he did talk above their humble strain,
And, as he knew that Nature had supply'd
What Fortune had deny'd him for Attraction,
Claim'd my weak Heart, and said he must possess it.

BARINA
Sure, they've put off this melancholy Meeting
Design'd in Honour of their lost Protector,
In which our share (tho' secret) must be greatest.
I see none move, nor hear their mournful Notes.

HERMINIA
Be not impatient: Where can we be better?
Have I not heard thee say sometimes, Barina,
That in a Dream, form'd by the Day's discourse
Of the sweet Life, that here they led in safety,
My Mother saw me wed one of these Swains,
And smil'd, tho' I had made a Choice below me?

BARINA
She did; and therefore never wou'd consent
That you, like others, shou'd behold their Revels:
Nor have I, since her Death left you my Charge,
Allow'd it, till worse Dangers forc'd us hither;
Tho' of myself, I ne'er observe such Trifles,

HERMINIA
D'ye call those nightly Visions then but Trifles?

BARINA
No doubt our Dreams are so; the work of Phancy,
Where things of Yesterday are odly piec'd
With what had pass'd some twenty Years before,
Knit in a weak and disproportion'd Chain,
Which cannot hold to lead us to the Future.
Whate'er I've said, I wish this had no meaning,
[Aside.
And that some other Place cou'd give us shelter.

HERMINIA
We'll walk a while–
Great Aristomenes, now cou'd I meet thee!
But that's a Blessing which I must not know,
[Aside.
'Till where thine is, my Spirit too shall go.
Oh! that my Grief wou'd force it to retire,
And Tears for him quench this new-kindl'd Fire!

[They go off the Stage.

[Enter at the other Door **CLIMANDER**.

CLIMANDER
Either my Eyes, indulgent to my Love,
Deceive my Hopes; or now, within their reach
That unknown Beauty moves, which lately charm'd them.
'Tis she! and with the speed that suits my Passion,
I will o'ertake, and farther urge it to her.

[Exit.

[Re-enter **HERMINIA**.

HERMINIA
She fears my Fate and fain wou'd have me go,
Before th' assembling Shepherds are arriv'd;
And having met one that can give her tydings,
Is busy to enquire about their coming.
Untimely Caution! —
—'Tis too late to move,
When once o'ertaken by the wings of Love.

[Enter **CLIMANDER** behind her.

CLIMANDER
From those fair Lips no sooner fell that word,
But all the neighb'ring Ecchoes caught the Sound,
And sent it doubl'd to Climander's Bosom:
The am'rous Streams have borne it down their Banks,
And the glad Plains breathe nothing, since, but Love.
Oh! speak it once again, and the fond Vine
Shall with a stricter grasp embrace the Elm,
Whilst joyful Birds shall hail it from the Branches.

HERMINIA
No; I have spoke too much—
Since on these Plains no syllable is secret.
Hereafter my close Thoughts shall be confin'd,
And in this Breast lock'd up from all Men's Knowledge.

CLIMANDER
Oh! not if Love be there; it cannot be:
Silence can ne'er last long, nor yet conceal it,
A thousand ways 'twill speak without a Voice,
And, whilst it struggles to obtain that Freedom,
Betraying Sighs will 'scape, and more declare it;
'Twill speak in list'ning to the Lover's Tale,
And say, 'tis Sympathy that makes it pleasant.

HERMINIA
He shakes my Soul, whilst thus he do's describe it:
For all he speaks I feel, and he must find.
[Aside.
Oh! yet, let me reflect upon my Birth,
And quit, in time, the Ground I can't maintain!

[She's going.

CLIMANDER
Nay, do not fly me, and I will be Speechless:
For if I speak, whilst on your Eyes I gaze,
It must be all of Love, and that offends you;

Yet since, perhaps, I ne'er may meet your more,
I wou'd have told the Story of my Heart,
And e'er it breaks, have mov'd you to Compassion.

HERMINIA
Meet him no more! then, what can Crowns afford me,
Amidst the noisie Pomp, that waits their Lustre?
Still shou'd I vainly listen for the Sound
[Aside.
Of such soft Words which charm my Sorrows from me.
Oh! that our Births were equal, as our Thoughts!
Yet I will pity him, and Fate be guilty.

[She stops and turns towards him.

CLIMANDER
Blest be the Thought, that thus retards your steps,
And turns again those gentle Lights upon me!
If Pity 'twas; Oh! yet indulge that warmth,
And Love 'twill soon produce, to meet my Wishes.

[She looks kindly on him.

'Tis done, 'tis done! be witness ye still skies,
That all her Looks are calm, and smooth as yours,
And not one Frown forbids my forward Hopes:
Let this fair Hand be added to confirm them,
And ease the mighty longings of my Passion.

[Kneels and kisses her Hand.

HERMINIA
Take, freely take this first and last of Favours.
Now, Shepherd rise, and hear what I've to say;
And if a Sigh mix with the fatal Sentence,
Believe, 'tis from the Grief, with which I give it.
You must not love me–

[She sighs.

CLIMANDER
I must not love you, tho' you Sigh to speak it!
Shou'd Pan pronounce it, in a Voice so loud
'Twou'd rive the knotty Oaks, that shade his Altars,
I wou'd to Syrinxes oppose your Beauties,
And ask the Gods, whose Loves had best Foundation?

HERMINIA
Those Gods, who made our Births so disproportion'd,
Wou'd say, they ne'er design'd our Hands shou'd join.
But see! the Swains are gath'ring tow'rds this Place:

Yet, Shepherd, know that if a Prince wou'd Love,
'Tis in your Form he must successful prove.

[Enter **ARCASIUS** with a Casket.

CLIMANDER
Then in this happy Form, since you approve it,
Behold—

[She interrupts him.

HERMINIA
No more! as you wou'd keep th' Esteem I've shown you.

[Exit.

CLIMANDER
Another time must tell this Secret to her.
Th' Ambition of her Mind charms like her Person,
[Aside.
Nor can the Blood, that breeds such Thoughts be abject.
But welcome good Arcasius with that Bait,
Which shall be soon dispers'd among the Soldiers:
And if it win them to my great Design,
'Tis worth the Kingdoms which its Price might ransom.

[Exeunt with the Casket follow'd by **ARCASIUS**.

[Enter **THÆTA** and **LAMIA**

LAMIA
The Dews are falling, and the Sun declin'd,
Whilst from this neighb'ring Grove are heard the Notes
Of that sweet Bird, that warbles to the Night,
Now telling us her Shadows are approaching:
And yet the tardy Shepherds are not come.

THÆTA
When all our Hours were gay, it was not thus:
But who can haste to break his chearful Pipe,
Tear the sweet Garland, made by her he sighs for,
And sing of Death, when Love is all his Passion?

LAMIA
Now thou dost talk of Love, yet ere we part,
Or fall into our melancholy Strains,
Lend to that Eccho, greedy of thy Voice,
Some moving Words, upon so soft a subject.

THÆTA
Rather that Song I'd chuse, which do's prefer

To all things else the Joys of these sweet Plains;
Since, now perhaps, we must too soon forsake them.

LAMIA
A better can't be chose; haste to perform it,
Lest the sad Ceremony break our purpose.

THE SONG
(I.)
She Sings.
A young Shepherd his Life,
    In soft Pleasure still leads,
    Tunes his Voice to his Reed,
    And makes Love in the Shades.
To be Great, to be Wise,
    To be Rich, to be Proud,
To be loaded with Bus'ness
    Or lost in a Croud,
He ne'er seeks, or desires:
    Let but Silvia be won,
He is Great, he is Rich,
    And his Bus'ness is done.

(II.)
    Whilst their Nymphs are as happy,
      As Happy as Fair;
For who has most Beauty,
    Has of Lovers most share.
Some will stay, some will fly,
    Some be false, some be true:
For the Lost we ne'er grieve,
    But still cherish the New. [Shouts.
'Tis vain of their Frailties,
    Or Falsehoods to mind 'em:
Mankind we must take,
    We must take, as we find 'em.

THÆTA
What Shouts are these!

[Shouts.

LAMIA
They're loud, and speak some Joy; and still repeated.

[Enter **HERMINIA** and **BARINA**.

LAMIA
Fair Stranger, know you whence these Shouts proceed?

HERMINIA

I do not; but these coming, sure, can tell us.

[Enter with great Signs of Joy **CLINIAS** with other **SHEPHERDS** and **SHEPHERDESSES**, &c.

CLINIAS
Swell, swell, Panisus, o'er thy spacious Bounds,
Flow like our Joy, and chear the Meads about thee.
Pan, take in thankful Sacrifice; our Flocks,
And ev'ry rural Swain proclaim his Praises!

LAMIA
Such Sounds, as these, meet with a gen'ral welcome:
But yet, the Cause we wish to hear explain'd.
Good Clinias, tell the Cause—

CLINIAS
He is return'd, and stands, like Fate, amongst 'em,
The Plain's Protector, and the Army's Genius,
The Virgin's Refuge, when the Town's in Flames,
And Shield to those whom Fortune makes his Vassals.

HERMINIA
'Tis Aristomenes thou hast described:
No other e'er cou'd fill a Praise like this.

CLINIAS
'Tis He indeed, next to the Gods, our Succour.

HERMINIA
Transporting News! how did the Army meet him?

CLINIAS
Just as a long stopt Current meets the sea,
And rushes on, when once't has forc'd a Passage.

2nd SHEPHERD
Heav'n has their Plumes; for high as that they toss 'em:
And not a dusty Soldier in the Host,
That has not hugged him to his swarthy Bosom.

CLINIAS
No Voice is what it was an Hour ago;
And their hoarse Joy sounds like their distant Drums;
His Hands, as if the Cretan Thongs still held them,
Are useless made, and fetter'd now with Kisses;
Whilst neighing Steeds think that the War surrounds them,
And prance in Air light as their Master's Minds.

2nd SHEPHERD
How he escap'd, all ask in such Confusion,
That their loud Questions drive his Answers back,

And will not let them reach the nearest to him.

HERMINIA
It is enough, ye Powers that guard Messenia!
We now must change our Habits, and return.
[Aside to **BARINA**
What did I say, return! O yes, I must,
And never hope to see Climander more:
[To herself
Yet will I give my Heart this last Relief
(Since Fate will have it bear th' unequal Passion)
To let him know my Love, and endless Flight,
And live on the dear Thought that he laments it.

[Exit with **BARINA**

LAMIA
Where is Aristor? Is he too return'd?

CLINIAS
That question did the Gen'ral ask aloud;
And 'twas the only one that cou'd be heard:
But no reply was made; I think he is not.

THÆTA
Then we're but half restor'd—
For he so heavily will take that Loss,
Our Joys will not be long, nor he amongst us.

LAMIA
Fear not the worst—

2nd SHEPHERD
I met a rumour of a stranger Prince,
That with large Sums new fir'd the trembling Host,
And from the Camp had led on some Design
A Party, that for Wealth wou'd risque their Lives,
Tho' cold and dull to Thoughts of gen'rous Duty.

CLINIAS
'Tis true; of Rhodes they say,
And some I heard that call'd him Demagetus.
Thick flew his Gold, as swarms of Summer-Bees,
And 'twas to succor or revenge the Gen'ral.
He asked their Aid—
But whither he has lead them, none can tell.
Ere Aristomenes return'd, he went
And is not heard of since.

2nd SHEPHERD
The Gen'ral's safe, and that's enough for us:

Now therefore Clinias, you that guide our Sports,
Tell us what we're to do to shew our Joy.

CLINIAS
To Laugh, to Sing, to Dance, to Play,
To rise with new appearing Day;
And ere the Sun has kiss'd 'em dry,
With various Rubans Nosegays tye.
Deckt with Flow'rs and cloath'd in Green,
Ev'ry Shepherdess be seen:
Ev'ry Swain with Heart and Voice
Meet him, meet him, and rejoice:
With redoubl'd Pæans sing him,
To the Plains, in Triumph bring him:
And let Pan and Mars agree,
That none's so kind and brave as He.

[Exeunt.

ACT IV

SCENE I

The General's Pavilion.

Enter Drest in the Habit of an Officer **DEMAGETUS** with **ARCASIUS**.

DEMAGETUS
Sh' has left the Plains, and is not to be found.
How cou'd'st thou bring this cruel Story to me,
Ere thou had'st search'd Messenia's utmost Bound,
And travell'd o'er the spacious World of Shepherds?
She must be yet amongst their Shades conceal'd;
And thro' them will I pierce, like prying Phoebus,
To find my Love, or lose myself for ever.

ARCASIUS
You will not hear (so much your Passion sways)
The Reasons, why I chose to see you first,
Ere I proceeded to pursue her Paths.

DEMAGETUS
There spoke the sixty Winters, that have froze thee,
And turn'd swift eager Love to Icy Reasons.
I must be Cold as thou art, if I hear thee,
Or lose one moment more in doating Questions.

[He's going.

ARCASIUS
Behold these Tokens, and let them retard you.

DEMAGETUS
Tokens of Love, sent to the fond Climander.
Oh! thou hast found a way indeed to stay me.

ARCASIUS
Take that, to you directed;

[A Letter.

And 'twas my Hopes from thence of some Discovery,
That kept me here 'till you had broke and read it.

DEMAGETUS
Then thou shalt hear it.
[Reads the Direction.
This to Climander from the Nymph that leaves him
To everlasting Grief, shou'd have been added,
For so 'twill prove, if no more Comfort's here.
[He reads it.
To love, yet from the Object fly,
Harder is, than 'tis to Dye:
Yet, for ever I remove,
Yet, for ever will I love.
Shepherd, seek no more to find;
Fate, not I, has been Unkind.
We pluck on Fate, by striving to avoid it.
To shun the low Addresses of a Swain,
For ever has she left a Prince despairing.
Why didst thou not, as I at parting bid thee,
Find out, and let her know my fair Intentions,
And that my Birth was Noble as her Wishes?

ARCASIUS
I was not negligent, nor wou'd be thought so:
But full of Transports when I heard your Story,
Thinking the Fates wou'd now fulfill their Promise
Thro' her the Daughter to the best of Men,
Fled to discover what you gave in Charge,
Travers'd the Plains in a long fruitless Search,
But cou'd not find that Beauty born to Bless us.

DEMAGETUS
I shew'd thee, as we pass'd, her new rais'd Hamlet.

ARCASIUS
Thither at last I went, but Oh! too late:
For ere I reach'd it, the fair Guest was vanish'd;
Upon the Floor lay her neglected Hook,

And o'er the Door hung Boughs of fading Willow,
To shew, as Shepherds use, the Place forsaken.
That Paper there I found, and near it lay,
This precious Gemm, that bears a well-cut Signet.

[Shews him a Ring.

By chance sure dropt, yet may assist your Purpose.

DEMAGETUS
Give me that Emblem of my fatal Passion:
For without End is that, as is this Circle.
Oh! that my way to Bliss shou'd seem so plain,
Yet in a moment thus be lost and wilder'd!
Now in the midst of Crouds and loud Applauses,
That greet me for restoring them Aristor,
Must wretched Demagetus sigh for Love,
And hang his drooping Head tho' wreathed with Laurels.

[A sound of Drums and Trumpets.

But hark! the Gen'ral comes—
To him the Oracle I have reveal'd,
And all the Story of my rural Life.
I'll tell him too the Cause of my new Grief,
Which to relieve, I instantly must leave him.

[A FLOURISH.

[Enter **ARISTOMENES**, **ARISTOR**, **ALCANDER**, and other **ATTENDANTS**.

ARISTOMENES
Why, Demagetus, art thou from my Sight,
From these fond Arms, that ever thus wou'd hold thee!

[Embracing him.

Thou kind Restorer of my lov'd Aristor.
Come to the Camp, and hear them shout thy Name,
Whilst I declare thee equal in Command
With him, who owes his Life to thy young Valour.

DEMAGETUS
Alas! my Lord—

ARISTOMENES
A Soldier sigh, when courting Fame attends him!
I know you Love, by your own kind Confession:
But that too must succeed, since now your Birth
Is known to answer all the great Desires,
Which, to my Wonder, did possess the Breast

Of that fair rural Maid, whose Beauty charm'd you.
We'll send, and with the Pomp that suits a Princess,
Since such your gen'rous Passion means to make her)
Have her conducted to a rich Pavilion,
And join your Hands, as Heav'n has join'd your Hearts.
This, my Aristor, be your pleasing Task.

[Enter an **ATTENDANT** to **ARISTOMENES**.

ATTENDANT
The Princess is without, and waits your Pleasure.

ARISTOMENES
Conduct her in–
[To **ALCANDER**.
I sent for her, to see the generous Stranger.

[Enter behind the Company **HERMINIA** and **BARINA**.

ARISTOR [To **ARISTOMENES**]
My Lord, what you command I take in charge.
[To **DEMAGETUS**.
Tell me, my best of Friends, the way to serve you.

DEMAGETUS
 I know it not my self, and that's the Torture.
Hear me, my Lord, nor think my Sorrows light:
[To **ARISTOMENES**.
For Love, the only Comfort of fond Youth,
Is lost for ever to the poor Climander.

HERMINIA
Climander –
That Name and Voice bears down my fainting Spirits.
I shall be known, yet have not Strength to fly:
Where shall this end, and where's Herminia's Honour!
    [To herself.

ARISTOMENES
So sad a Pause still keeps us in Suspence:
Proceed, and if there's help on Earth, we'll find it.

DEMAGETUS
At my return, made joyful by Success,
With hasty Steps, and in my Heart soft Wishes,
Love, and a thousand flatt'ring Expectations,
I fled the clam'rous Praise prepar'd to meet me,
And sought the Path that led to my Desires:
But ere I was advanc'd beyond the Camp,
The Voice of this Old Man
Cross'd my sad way, and cry'd, She's gone for ever.

ARISTOMENES
Perhaps 'tis some Mistake,
If other Proofs are wanting to confirm it.

DEMAGETUS
Oh! far too many for Climander's Peace.
She own'd her Love, and with this Signet bound it,
And in the Folds of this dear Paper left
At once the tokens of my Joy and Ruin.

[Gives the Letter and Ring to **ARISTOMENES**.

HERMINIA
The Character and Signet will betray me;
And now Necessity must make me Bold.
[Aside.
Oh! yet, ere you proceed to view that Paper,

[She throws herself at **ARISTOMENE'S** Feet.

(Wrapt in Confusion) hear your Daughter speak,

[As he is opening the Letter.

And pity in her Fate all Women's Frailty.

ARISTOMENES
Ha! Thou dost much surprize me; but go on,
And, 'till she has finish'd, let no Word be utter'd.

DEMAGETUS
By all my fleeting Sorrows 'tis my Love:
Nor cou'd I, but to hear her speak, be Silent.
    [Aside.

ARISTOMENES
Proceed, and 'bate those Tears, that stay thy Speech.

HERMINIA
That I have stoop'd below the Blood you gave me,
And cast my doating Love upon that Shepherd,
(For such he is, altho' a Plume adorns him)
My wretched Hand, and now my Tongue confesses:
For by that Paper, indiscreetly penn'd,
The Secret wou'd be told, shou'd I conceal it.
But Oh! my Lord, since you can ne'er forgive me;
A sad Recluse for ever let me live,
Or Dye for Love, to do my Birth more Justice.

ARISTOMENES

Be comforted, and farther yet unfold
How first you came acquainted with this Shepherd.

HERMINIA
To 'scape the Fury of prevailing Foes,
Disguised, I in your absence sought the Plains,
And in that Habit heard the pow'rful Sighs
Of one that knew not then his own Presumption.

ARISTOMENES
Were he a Prince, and still wou'd urge his Suit
Wou'd'st thou receive 't, and bless the Pow'rs that sent him?

HERMINIA
I shou'd not hide my Thoughts, or blush to own them.
Yes, I cou'd bless those Pow'rs which now undo me.

[**DEMAGETUS** comes forward.

DEMAGETUS
I cannot wait these Forms; Love plead my Pardon,
When, Sir, I disobey your order'd Silence,
And haste to tell her 'tis a Prince adores her,
That wou'd have sought her on the lowly Plains,
And for her Favour quitted all Dominion.

ARISTOMENES
Then take her, thou most worthy Prince of Rhodes!

[Giving her to him.

And know, Herminia, to encrease thy Passion,
Thou hold'st that noble Hand, that sav'd thy Brother,
And gives thy Father, in this new Alliance,
More Joy than when he first receiv'd and bless'd thee.

DEMAGETUS
Let all the Joys of Earth give place to mine,
Whilst in deep, silent Raptures I possess them:

[Taking her from **ARISTOMENES**.

For Demagetus is above Discourse,
And will not wrong his Love with faint Expressions.

HERMINIA
So let mine flow, and O Barina, see
I smiling give my Hand now to a Shepherd,
Yet fear not to offend my Mother's Ghost.

BARINA

No; that smiles too, and all that love and serve you.

ARCASIUS
The Fate of Rhodes is clear and chearful now;
And old Arcasius has outliv'd his Cares.

ARISTOR
Now as a Brother, take this new Embrace;
[To **DEMAGETUS**.
Tho' all the Love, it shews, you had before.

ARISTOMENES
Conduct her, Demagetus, to her Tent:
I'll soon be there, and see those Rites perform'd,
That shall confirm her Yours; be Kind and Happy.

[Exeunt **HERMINIA** and **DEMAGETUS** leading her follow'd by **ARCASIUS**, **BARINA** and **OTHERS**. **ARISTOR** is going too but is call'd back by his **FATHER**.

Come back Aristor, and the rest withdraw:
For something I wou'd say to you in private.

[The **ATTENDANTS** go off.

Free from the Croud, and unobserv'd my Transports,
I wou'd embrace, and welcome thee to Life,
And with a loud repeated Blessing pay
The pious Care, that brought it to such Dangers.
Oh! that the Love of Women shou'd be thought
To pass the Fondness which a Father feels,
When thus he grasps a Son of thy Perfections,

[Embracing him.

My Dear, my Lov'd Aristor!

ARISTOR
My Prince, my Gen'ral, and the Best of Fathers!

ARISTOMENES
Thy Heart speaks loud, and knocking at my Breast
Seems as 'twou'd close in conference with mine.

ARISTOR
It wou'd, my Lord, and strives to force its Passage.

[**ARISTOMENES** looses his Arms from embracing him.

ARISTOMENES
Oh, no my Son! for now I must be plain,
And tell thee, thou dost lock some Secret there

Which all my depth of Kindness ne'er cou'd fathom:
I see it in the Cloud, that shades thy Brow.
And still thy pensive Eyes are downwards cast,
As thou wou'd'st seek the Grave, or something lower:
Long have I this observed—
And thought whole Nights away to find the Cause,
Which now, my Son, I urge thee to reveal:
And think that He who best can love thee asks it.

ARISTOR
Oh! that you did not love, or wou'd not ask it!
I cannot speak, for speaking must offend:
Yet shou'd my Silence grieve such mighty Goodness,

'Twou'd break that Heart, which thus you seek to succour.
Upon my Knees a strange Request I make,

[Offering to Kneel but his **FATHER** takes him up.

That you wou'd quite forget and think me Dead;
Which the approaching Battle shou'd confirm,
And leave you to possess your other Comforts.

ARISTOMENES
My other Comforts! All are light to Thee:
And when I wou'd have shar'd amongst my Race
Impartial Kindess, as their Birthrights claim'd,
Still to my Heart Aristor wou'd be nearest,
Still, with a Merit not to be withstood,
Wou'd press beyond my cool and equal Purpose,
And seize a double Portion of my Love:
And wilt thou lose it now, to keep thy Silence?

ARISTOR [Sighs]
My Life I rather wou'd; but Oh! my Lord!

ARISTOMENES
Another Sigh, another yet, my Son!
And then, let Words relieve this mighty Passion:
They will, they will; the Sweetness of thy Temper
Will melt before a just and warm Persuasion.
Now, let me know it—

ARISTOR
Believe that it 'twere fit, it shou'd be told:
But Oh! my Lord, 'tis what you must not know.

ARISTOMENES
Not I, Aristor! if thy Soul were bare
As is thy faded Cheek now to thy Father,
It were most fit—

Oh! think, my Son, who 'twas that made it Noble,
And train'd it in the Paths of Truth and Honour:
Else, what had hinder'd, but thou might'st have been
(In spite of all the Virtues with thee born,
For Education is the stronger Nature)
A bragging Coward, or a base Detractor,
A Slave to Wealth, or false to Faith or Friendship
Lull'd in the common Arms of some Seducer,
And lost to all the Joys of Virtuous Love.

ARISTOR
Ha! Virtuous Love!

ARISTOMENES
What, dost thou start? why, so I meant thou shou'dst.
When hastily I press'd that Word upon thee,
To catch that flushing Witness in thy Face,
Was all this Bait contriv'd; no more, my Son,
No more dissembling of a Truth so plain:
I see 'tis Love, the best of all our Passions.
And fram'd like Thee; sure none cou'd e'er Despair,
Nor can I fear thou'd'st make a vulgar Choice.

ARISTOR
On Ida's Top not Paris made a nobler,
When of three Goddesses he chose the Fairest.

ARISTOMENES
Will she not hear thy Love?

ARISTOR
Oh yes! with all the softness of her Sex,
And answers it with Vows, more strong than Ours.

ARISTOMENES
If thus it be, what hast thou then to fear?

ARISTOR
A Father's Wrath, more dreadful to Aristor
Than is the frown of Jove, that shakes the Poles,
And makes the Gods forget they are Immortal.

ARISTOMENES
Thou wrong'st my Love in that mistaken Terror.
By all those Powers I swear, I will not cross thee;
Be she a Spartan Dame, 'bate me but One,
And tho' a Foe, I yield thou shou'd'st possess her.

ARISTOR
I dare not ask; my trembling Love forbids it.
Who is that One, so fatally excepted?

ARISTOMENES
Then, I'll by telling thee prevent that Trouble.
It is the Tyrant Anaxander's Daughter,
Whom, tho' I ne'er beheld, I must abhor,
As borrowing her Blood from such a Fountain.

ARISTOR
Take mine, my Lord, then to wash out that Stain

[Offers his Breast.

You'll think it has contracted by her Love:
For 'tis that Tyrant's Daughter I adore,
And ne'er, while Life is here, will change my Purpose.

ARISTOMENES
Confusion seize those Words, and Her that caus'd 'em!
Not Groans of Earthquakes, or the Burst of Thunder,
The Voice of Storms urging the dang'rous Billows,
E'er struck the Sense with sounds of so much Horror.
It must not, Oh! it must not, shall not be:
Sooner this Dagger, tho' my Soul lives in thee,

[Drawing **AMALINTHA'S** Dagger.

Shou'd let out thine with this prepost'rous Passion.
Than I wou'd yield, it e'er shou'd meet Success.

ARISTOR
Of all the Instruments by Vulcan form'd,
That Poinard best is fitted to my Heart,
Since Her's it was, whose Eyes have deeper pierc'd it:
Quickly, my Lord, let me receive it here,
And see me proud in Death to wear that Favour.

[**ARISTOMENES** amaz'd looks on the Dagger, and speaks to himself.

ARISTOMENES
This Dagger Her's, this Anaxander's Daughter's!
Fate then is practicing upon my Soul
What sudden Turns and Tryals Man can bear.

ARISTOR
Oh! do not pause—
Lest fainting with the Weight of what I feel,
I poorly fall, unlike your Son or Soldier.

ARISTOMENES
If this were Her's, Her's were the grateful Vows,
With which I rashly charg'd the Life she gave me.

[Still to himself.

ARISTOR
Ha! not a Look, not one sad parting Word!
Then my own Hand thus sets me free for ever.

[Offers to Stab himself, but is stay'd by **ARISTOMENES**.

ARISTOMENES
Hold! by Love and Duty yet a moment hold!

ARISTOR
My Life they've sway'd, and must command a Moment
But let it not exceed, lest both I cancel,
And only listen to my wild Despair.

ARISTOMENES
Shall I perform them? shall I hear her plead?
And to a Woman's Claim resign my Vengeance?
No; let my Ear still fly the fatal Suit,
And from her Tears be turn'd my harden'd Face.
What did I say! a hasty Blush has seized it,
For but imagining a Thing so vile.
Turn back my Face from Her that shunn'd not mine,
When it was Death to know, and to preserve me!
No; let the Fiends be obstinate in Ill,
Revenge be their's, while Godlike Man is grateful.

[Enter an **ATTENDANT**.

ATTENDANT
Pardon, my gracious Lord, this bold Intrusion.
Two Ladies veil'd, escaping from Phærea,
Ask with such earnestness for Prince Aristor,
That, sure, their Bus'ness is of mighty Moment.
From one this Ring at her entreaty, Sir, I must deliver.

[Gives it to **ARISTOR** and Exit.

ARISTOMENES
Retire, and if not call'd, return no more.

ARISTOR
'Tis Amalintha's Ring, my Amalintha's:
She's come in time, to see me fall her Victim.

ARISTOMENES
No; to receive her from from my Hand, my Son;
Since 'twas from her's, I took this healing Weapon,
That has cut off the Hate in which I held her.
'Twas she that met me rising from my Grave,

And fearless freed the Foe to her and Sparta:
Then in a grateful Promise was I bound
Not to deny whate'er she shou'd request;
And sure thy Love, before the Pomp of Crowns,
Is what a Maid must ask, that knows its Value.

ARISTOR
The Transports of my Soul be thus exprest;
Then let me Dye, for having griev'd such Goodness.

[Embracing his Father's Knees.

ARISTOMENES
No; rise my Son, go meet and chear thy Love,
And to this Tent conduct the Royal Maid,
Whilst in that inner Part I stand conceal'd,
And hear her tell why thus she comes to seek us:
Thence will I issue, as occasion calls,
And giving thee, give all I hold most precious.

[He goes into the inner Tent. **ARISTOR** goes out at the other Door and re-enters immediately leading **AMALINTHA** veil'd follow'd by **PHILA**

ARISTOR
Dismiss that Cloud, and with it all your Fears,
Safe in this Camp, and in Aristor's Love,
Which ne'er was truly bless'd, 'till this glad Moment.
Now Amalintha, let my Joys o'erflow;
And ere I ask what brought thee to my sight,
Let it be filled with thy amazing Beauties,
And with this Hand my longing Lips be clos'd.

[Kisses her Hand.

AMALINTHA
Thus, after each short absence, may we meet,
Thus pleas'd, thus wrapt in Love, thus dying fond.
But Oh Aristor! since I last beheld you,
So has this Life been threaten'd by the Fates,
That to your Arms 'tis forc'd for Peace and Safety.

ARISTOR
Still may they prove a Haven for my Love,
Too strong for all the Shocks of rig'rous Fortune.
But what beneath thy Father's Roof cou'd fright thee?
Or what bold Danger break thro' his Protection?

AMALINTHA
'Twas from Himself, and all the Lords of Sparta.
When Aristomenes they found escap'd,
High was their Rage as Billows in a Tempest;

And all the Arts of State were put in use
To find who had assisted in his Flight:
But still in vain, 'till subtle, vile Clarinthus –

ARISTOR
That Villain will be first in Blood and Mischief.
But cou'd he pry into thy generous Heart,
And find it there, that you had nobly done it?
And are not secret Thoughts secure against him?

AMALINTHA
I did believe them so, 'till he disprov'd it:
For 'twas his Counsel, when all others fail'd,
To know by speaking Gods the deep Contrivance;
And from the Oracle, in some few Moments,
The full Discov'ry will have reach'd Phærea.
Which ere it does, I was advis'd to leave,
By one that heard the horrid Voice accuse me,
And with a Speed unmark'd outflew the rest.

ARISTOR
As swiftly may the bounteous Gods reward him.

AMALINTHA
This, my Aristor, brings me to your Tents,
But not to save my Life, or 'scape their Fury:
For shou'd your Heart, which boldly I will claim,
Be yet deny'd me by your injur'd Father,
Not all his Army shou'd retard my Steps
From leading to the Town, and certain Ruin;
For they have sworn it (with this Imprecation,
That 'till 'tis done, no Victory may bless them)
To sacrifice the Soul that sav'd the Gen'ral.

[Enter **ARISTOMENES** from the inward Tent.

ARISTOMENES
That Army you have nam'd, shall first in Flames
Consume the utmost Town of Lacedemon.
Take your Security, and softest Wishes,
Your dear Aristor take, and if ought more
The fair Preserver of his Father claims,
Be it but nam'd, and at that instant granted.

AMALINTHA
Beyond Aristor's Heart there's no Request,
No longing Thought, no Hope for Amalintha:
For still his Love prescrib'd their tender Limits.

ARISTOR
Oh! let it not be thought irrev'rent Passion,

If in the awful Presence of a Father
I run upon my Joys, and grasp 'em thus.

[Embraces her.

ARISTOMENES
Thou well dost intimate I shou'd retire;
For Privacy is only fit for Lovers.

ARISTOR
Pardon my Transport, Sir, nor thus mistake it.

ARISTOMENES
No more, my Son! but when the Trumpet calls,
Which must be soon, remember thou'rt a Soldier,
And that the Battle, we shall lead to morrow,
Will ask our best of Care and Preparation.

ARISTOR
Never was I yet wanting to my Charge.
But give me leave here to attend that Summons.

[Exit **ARISTOMENES**.

For Oh! my Amalintha, since thou'rt mine,
Since I can tell my Heart that darling Truth;
The Moments that must take me from thy sight,
Will pass for lost, and useless to Aristor.
And this War done, which we now soon shall finish
(For You not there, what God will fight for Sparta?)
I'll swear the Sun and radiant Light shall part,
Ere I will once be found from this lov'd Presence.

AMALINTHA
Confirm it, all ye soft and gentle Pow'rs!
And let the pattern of a Love so perfect
Reform Mankind, and bless believing Women.
But can I think it is Aristor speaks?
That I behold, and hear you safe from Danger,
Whom late I saw assaulted so with Death,
When from the Guard a Weapon you had snatched,
And but that brave Swords length cou'd keep him from you?
Hope and fond Expectation all had left me:
Arm'd with this Dagger full I stood in vain,
And from my Window watch'd the fatal Stroke,
Which soon was to be copy'd on my Heart;
Then, had I meant to own your noble Love,
And told mine Dying, whilst the Croud had trembl'd.

ARISTOR
I saw your dire Intent, and that preserv'd me:

For 'twas to stop your Arm, that mine perform'd
What else had been above the Force of Nature;
And when the Drums of Demagetus thunder'd,
As thro' the shiver'd Gates he rush'd to save me,
You may remember, that I wou'd not meet him,
Till I had told my Love what meant the Tumult,
Which since has given me Fears, cold as pale Death,
Lest some Observer might have charg'd it on you.

[Trumpets sound.

AMALINTHA
No; for too much their own Concern engag'd them.
But Oh! already hark! the Trumpet calls,
And jealous Fame no longer lets me keep you.
Must you be gone, must you obey this Summons?

ARISTOR
Oh! yes, I must; it is the Voice of Honour.
Yet, do not weep–
Be this Embrace the Earnest of a Thousand.
Now let me lead you to Herminia's Tent
Then think, I go more to secure your Charms,
And fight to rest with Peace in these fair Arms.

[He leads her off.

ACT V

SCENE I

The **SCENE** is the Camp. A Noise of Drums and Trumpets.

Enter **ARISTOMENES, ARISTOR, DEMAGETUS, ALCANDER, SEVERAL OFFICERS** and **SOLDIERS**.

Enter an **OFFICER** from the other Door, and speaks to the **GENERAL**.

OFFICER
My Lord! I'm from Alcander bid to say,
The Battle he has marshall'd as you order'd;
And that your Presence now is only wanted.

ARISTOMENES
Tell him we come; and let the Drums beat higher.
Now, my brave Followers, be your selves to Day,
And more I need not ask, that know your Valour;
Who've seen you at the backs of Spartans ride,
Till their long Flight, and not your Conquest, tir'd you.

[The **SOLDIERS** shout.

And Oh! my Sons, since they who bravely seek it,
May meet with Death, when all his Darts are flying,
Let me Embrace, and breathe my Blessings on ye.

[Embraces **DEMAGETUS**.

Yet, Demagetus, if I 'scape him now,
And Victory attends my great Endeavour,
Thou shalt Triumphant lead me into Rhodes,
Where we'll obey the Gods, and save thy Country.

DEMAGETUS
Still you're the Best of Men, as they declar'd you.

ARISTOMENES
Now let me fold thee thus, my Life's best Treasure!

[He embraces **ARISTOR**, but seems disorder'd, and not to feel him in his Arms, which he often clasps about him.

Thou dost not fill my Arms, 'tis Air I grasp:
Nor do my Eyes behold thee—
Where is my Son, ha! where is my Aristor?

ARISTOR
 Here my dear Lord, here pressing to your Bosom.

[His Voice seems to **ARISTOMENES** (still under his disorder) to be low and different to what it was usually.

ARISTOMENES
From what far distant Valley comes thy Voice?
It seems so hollow, scarce my Ear receives it.

ARISTOR
What means my noble Father!

ARISTOMENES
Till now, my faithful Senses never fail'd me.
They talk of Omens, ha! I must not think on't;
Such chilling Damps wou'd blast a Day of Battle:
[Aside.
Yet let my evil Genius but be true,
And a fam'd End is all it can portend me.

ARISTOR
You reason with your self, and turn from us.
May we not know what thus disturbs your Thoughts?

ARISTOMENES
Nothing—a Vapour crossed me, but 'tis gone:
And now the Field, the dusty Field, my Sons,
Must be the Scene, where we shall nobly act
What our great Spirits, and our Country urges.
The Trumpet calls, with the impatient Drum;
And He that loves his Honour, let him come.

[He draws his Sword and goes off follow'd by the rest with their Swords drawn, Drums and Shouts of Battle immediately succeed.

[The Noise continues, the **SCENE** changes to a fine Tent.

[Enter **AMALINTHA** follow'd by **PHILA**.

ARISTOMENES
Not yet enough! when will this Discord end!
Is there no happy Land,
Where only Love, and its kind Laws prevail?
Where the false Trumpet flatters not to Death,
Nor the more noisy Drum outcries the Dying?
Oh! Phila, why shou'd Men with Hearts unmov'd
Seek the bold War, and leave ours trembling for them?
Now whilst I speak, a chilling Fear surrounds me;
And ev'ry Tread I hear, is hast'ning on,
Methinks, to tell me, all my Hopes are perish'd.

PHILA
Why shou'd you, Madam, who have pass'd already,
Unhurt by Fortune, thro' more threat'ning Dangers,
Now faint, when Reason bids you think the best?
The Sound goes from us, and the lucky War
(Since you've the Promise of your Father's Life)
Proceeds, as we cou'd wish, for the Messenians.

AMALINTHA
So do's it seem; but yet my failing Spirits
Sink to my Heart, and bid it think of Ruin.
Last Night my Dreams shew'd me Aristor bleeding;
And o'er my Head a screaming Voice proclaim'd
That Amalintha's hasty Fate had kill'd him:
I clos'd my Eyes to catch another Vision,
That might interpret, or prevent the first;
But all in vain, no Help or Comfort found me,
And wrapt in Fears, I wak'd and still continue
For what's foretold so fatal to my Love.

PHILA
Your Fate work his? it rather will protect him.
But here come Tydings, and the Bearer smiles;
Good let them be, and these vain Fears will vanish.

[Enter an **OFFICER**.

AMALINTHA
From Prince Aristor? Do's he live, and send you?

OFFICER
Madam he does–
And bids me say, what I my self can witness,
That Lacedemon's Battle breaks to pieces,
And soon will give him leave to find you here.

AMALINTHA
Take this, and wear it, Soldier, for your News;

[Gives him a Jewel.

And may your Honours still outshine its Lustre.
Stay here, whilst I report this to Herminia,
If Demagetus too be yet in safety.

OFFICER
He is; and near Aristor did I leave him.

AMALINTHA
Come with me Phila; yet my Heart is heavy,
And wou'd be forcing Tears to my sad Eyes:
But I'll repel them with this welcome Message,
And put on all the smiles of Love to meet him.

[Exit with **PHILA** into the Tent.

OFFICER
The Centinels have all forsook the Tents,
In hopes to share the Plunder of the Foe,
Finding by their retiring we prevail:
But I'll report it loudly to the General.
Oh! here are some returning; are they Messenians?
They wear the Habit, yet no Face I know;
Their Haste and Looks do seem to point at Mischief:
I will conceal my self, and watch their Purpose.

[He conceals himself.

[Enter **CLARINTHUS** with others disguis'd like **MESSENIAN SOLDIERS**.

CLARINTHUS
You heard the King, and the chief Lords of Sparta
Wish, that no Victory might bless our Arms,
Till we had sacrificed the Traytor's Life,
That freed this Lyon, which devours us all.

SOLDIER
We did, we did—

CLARINTHUS
You've also heard, 'twas Amalintha's Action.

SOLDIER
Yes, and the King then said, his Vow shou'd stand:
And she had Dy'd, I think, had she not fled for't.

CLARINTHUS
'Tis true; therefore when I reflected on our Curse,
And saw that Conquest wou'd no more attend us
Till we perform'd what to the Gods we swore,
I mov'd the King—
To let me with your Aid attempt the Camp,
Which if I found unguarded,
I wou'd to Sparta soon convey the Traytress,
Where she shou'd meet the Rigour of the Law.
These are the Royal Tents, where she must be;
Therefore no more remains, but to secure her.

[They follow him into the inner Tent and the conceal'd **OFFICER** comes out.

OFFICER
Curst Conspiration, not to be prevented
With but my single Arm against their Numbers!
But to the Battle, and Aristor's Ear I'll fly for Help;
That may o'ertake, and cross the bloody Purpose.

[Exit.

[The **WOMEN** shriek in the inner Tent, and Re-enter **CLARINTHIA** &c. leading in **AMALINTHA** and **PHILA**.

AMALINTHA
Messenians are ye, and yet treat me thus!
Restrain those Hands, that gave your Gen'ral to you.
Let me but hear you speak, and name the Cause;
Which, if a just one, I'll submit to Fortune.

CLARINTHUS
'Tis but too just, and do's not ask explaining.

AMALINTHA
Oh! now Clarinthus in your Voice I read
The cruel Sentence of an angry Father.
Turn not away that Face, but hear your Princess;
I can't resist, no Force, no Help is near me:
Therefore command, that but my Arms be freed,

And let me not be dragg'd, where I must follow.

CLARINTHUS
Will you, relying then on me for Safety,
Forbear to cry for Help, as we conduct you?

AMALINTHA
By Castor's Soul I swear it.

CLARINTHUS
Then taking first her Dagger, free her Arms.
Give me your Hand, and now perform your Promise,
To follow where I'll lead you–

[Just as **CLARINTHUS** is offering to take her Hand, she snatches **PHILA'S** Dagger, and then answers **CLARINTHUS**.

AMALINTHA
No, stay Clarinthus; that I did not Promise.
My Voice, and not my Feet, my Word engag'd;
And whilst my Hand holds this, I will not follow.

CLARINTHUS
So swift and subtle? yet disarm and take her.

AMALINTHA
Hear me but speak, Clarinthus:
My Father's Life already I've secur'd;
And if you yet will quit this dang'rous Purpose,
Yours with Rewards, as great as your Desires,
Shall too be given you, and all Wrongs lie bury'd.

CLARINTHUS
More than I love Rewards, I hate Messenia;
Therefore alive or dead will bear you from 'em.

[He offers to seize her, she keeping him off with her Dagger kneels.

AMALINTHA
Oh! Pity yet my Youth, and wretched Fortunes;
A Princess at your Feet behold in Tears,
And Spare the Blood, the Royal Blood of Sparta.

CLARINTHUS
Yes, and be lost our selves to save a Trayt'ress?
For, such you've been to that high Blood you've boasted.
I will not spare nor pity, but thus seize you.

[He wrests the Dagger from her, she rises hastily and follow'd by **PHILA** escapes into the Tent, **CLARINTHUS** pursues her, and immediately the Cries of **WOMEN** are heard.

[Enter at the other Door **ARISTOR** and **SOLDIERS**.

ARISTOR
Oh! we are come in time. Detested Villains,
Your Deaths are all that you shall meet with here.

[They fight.

[Re-enter **CLARINTHUS**.

CLARINTHUS
The Victim's struck which could not be borne off.
Now my next Task
Must be to rescue those, who shar'd the Danger.

[He runs at **ARISTOR**, who kills him, he speaks falling.

Thou'st kill'd Clarinthus, And
The Fiends reward thee.

ARISTOR
Dye; and those Fiends thou call'st on meet thy Spirit.
I askt but that, to crown the War we've ended.

[He and his **MEN** fall on the rest, fighting off the Stage.

[Enter **AMALINTHA** wounded and supported by **PHILA**.

AMALINTHA
Phila thy Hand; help me to reach that Couch,
The dying Bed of wretched Amalintha!
Nay, do not weep, since 'tis the Fate's Decree,
Who let one luckless Moment interpose
Betwixt Aristor's coming, and my Ruin.
Here, set me down; and let this last Embrace

[Sits down.

Reward the Cares and Fears, my Life has cost thee.
Now leave me, Phila, to perform a Part
Which must not be prevented by thy Tears.

PHILA
Thus pale, thus faint, thus dying must I leave you!

AMALINTHA
Yes; if thou wilt obey, thou must retire.
But be not far, and when thou seest me fall'n
Dead in Aristor's Arms, who'll soon return,
Come forth, and tell him 'twas my last Request
(By all our Love, by all our Sighs and Sorrows,

By our new Vows, and swiftly faded Joys)
That He wou'd yet survive his Amalintha;
Nor let my fatal Vision prove a Truth,
That 'twas my Fate, my hasty Fate that kill'd him.

PHILA
Let me but stay, at least 'till he's arriv'd.

AMALINTHA
'Twou'd cross my Purpose, hark! I hear him coming.
Quickly retire and let me hide this Stream,
Lest he shou'd swell it with a Flood of Tears,
And waste in Grief my small remaining Life,
Which I design to lavish out in Love.

[**PHILA** goes off. **AMALINTHA** pulls her Garment over her Wound.

About him let my dying Arms be thrown,
Whilst I deny my parting Life one Groan.
My failing Breath shall in soft Sighs expire,
And tender Words spend my last vital Fire;
That of my Death Men this account may give,
She ceas'd to Love, as others cease to Live.

[Enter **ARISTOR** hastily, and sits down by her.

ARISTOR
How fares my Love? sink not beneath your Fears,
When this most lucky Hand has made them groundless,
Securing to my Life its greatest Blessing,
Your matchless Love and all its dying Transports.

AMALINTHA
Its dying Transports, did you say Aristor?
I wou'd be glad to know, that Death has Transports.
But are there none, none that do Live and Love?
That early meet, and in the Spring of Youth,
Uncross'd, nor troubl'd in the soft Design,
Set sweetly out, and travel on to Age
In mutual Joys, that with themselves expire?

ARISTOR
Indeed, there are but few, that are thus Happy.
But since our Lot it is, t'encrease the number;
Let us not lose a Thought on other's Fortunes,
But keep them still employ'd upon our own;
For in no Hearts, sure, Love e'er wrought more Wonders.

AMALINTHA
Oh! not, to mine I gladly did admit it
Thro' the stern hazards of a Father's Wrath,

And all the Hate of Sparta and Messenia.
If e'er I wept, 'twas Love that forc'd the Dew,
And not my Country, or my colder Friendships;
And on my Face (when Lacedemon mourn'd)
Suspected Smiles were seen to mock her Losses;
Because that Love was on the adverse Party.
Thus fond, thus doating have I pass'd my Hours,
And with their dear remembrance will I close
My Life's last Scene, and grasp you thus in Dying.

[She embraces him.

ARISTOR
Far be that Hour; but Oh! my Amalintha,
Proceed thus to describe thy tender Soul,
And charm me with thy might Sense of Passion;
For know, 'twas that which fix'd me ever thine,
When with a Pleasure, not to be express'd,
I found no Language of my Love escap'd thee,
Tho' wrapped in Myst'ry to delude the Croud;
When ev'ry longing Look cou'd raise a Blush,
And every Sigh I breath'd heave this lov'd Bosom,
Which held such soft Intelligence with mine,
And now o'erflows with a like Tide of Pleasure.

ARISTOR
Oh! yes it do's; it meets the vast Delight,
And takes the Thoughts ev'n of Elysium from me.
Nor will I, as some peevish Beauty might,
Take light offence, that mine you did not mention;
Since 'tis my equalling Aristor's Love
Is all the Charm, I wou'd be proud to boast of.

ARISTOR
Believe not, that I slighted such Perfections.
I saw you Fair, beyond the Fame of Helen;
But Beauty's vain, and fond of new Applause,
Leaving the last Adorer in Despair
At his approach, who can but praise it better:
Whilst Love, Narcissus-like, courts his Reflection,
And seeks itself, gazing on other's Eyes.
When this I found in yours, it bred that Passion,
Which Time, nor Age, nor Death, shall e'er diminish.

AMALINTHA
For Time, or Age, I think not of their Power.
But, after Death, Aristor, cou'd you love me,
Still call to me your Thoughts, when so far absent,
And mourn me sleeping in that Rival's Arms?

ARISTOR

Yes; if I cou'd outlive my Amalintha,
Still shou'd I turn my Eyes to that cold Grave,
Still love thee there, and wish to lie as low.
But why do's ev'ry Period of thy Speech
Thus sadly close with that too mournful Subject?
Why, now I press this Question, dost thou weep,
Yet in my Bosom strive to hide thy Tears?
Paleness is on thy Cheek, and thy damp Brow
Strikes to my Heart such sympathizing Cold,
As quenches all its Fire, but that of Love.
Oh! speak my Life, my Soul, my Amalintha;
Speak, and prevent the boding Fears that tell me
Eternal Separation is at hand,
And after this, I ne'er shall clasp thee more.

[Embraces her, and she starts and groans.

AMALINTHA
Oh! O', O', O'.

ARISTOR
Nay, if the gentle foldings of my Love,
The tender circling of these Arms can wound,
'Tis sure some inward Anguish do's oppress thee,
Which too unkindly thou wilt still keep secret.

AMALINTHA
Secret it shou'd have been, 'till Death had seal'd it;
Had not that Groan, and my weak Tears betray'd me:
[Speaks faintly.
For Death, which from Clarinthus I receiv'd,
Is come to snatch my Soul from these Embraces.

ARISTOR
Oh fatal sound! but let me not suppose it,
Till Art is weary'd for thy Preservation.
Haste to procure it Phila: all that hear me
Fly to her Aid; or you more speedy Gods
The Cure be yours, and Hecatombs attend you.
But none approach; then let me haste to bring it,
Tho' thus to leave her is an equal Danger.

[Endeavours to go.

AMALINTHA
Aristor stay; nor let my closing Eyes
One Moment lose the Sight that ever charm'd them.
No Art can bring relief; and melting Life
But lingers till my Soul receives th' Impression
Of that lov'd Form, which ever shall be lasting,
Tho' in new Worlds, new Objects wou'd efface it.

ARISTOR

No, Amalintha; if it must be so,
Together we'll expire, and trace those Worlds,
As fond, and as united as before:
For know, my Love the Sword of War has reach'd me;
And none wou'd I permit to bind the Wound,
Till to thy gentle Hand I cou'd reveal it.
The Blood uncheck'd shall now profusely flow,
And Art be scorn'd, that cou'd but half restore me.

AMALINTHA

Oh! let me plead in Death against that Purpose,
Employ my Hand, yet warm, to close the Wound,
And with my suppling Tears disperse the Anguish.
Your Country asks your stay, and more your Father:
This Blood is his, ally'd to all his Virtues,
By him more priz'd, than what supports his Frame,
Nor shou'd be lavish'd thus without his Licence.
Oh! Aristomenes haste to preserve it,
Since Life from me departs, and Love is useless
Aristor –

[She dies.

ARISTOR

Her fleeting Breath has borne far hence my Name:
But soon my following Spirit shall o'ertake her.
My Godlike Father gave her to my Arms,
And then resign'd to her more powerful Claim
This purple Stream, which wafts me to possess her.
May every Power, that shields paternal Goodness,
Enfold his Person, and support his Sway:
His dear remembrance take these parting drops,

[He weeps.

And then be free, my Soul, for ties more lasting,
Eternal Love, the faithful Lovers due,
In those blest Fields, which stand display'd before me.
My Amalintha–

[He takes her in his Arms and dies.

[Enter **PHILA**.

PHILA

I shou'd have come, and urg'd his Preservation,
If when I saw her fall my Strength had served me:
But all my Cares departed with her Life,
And mine I hope is now for ever going.

[She falls in a swoon at **AMALINTHA'S** feet.

[Shouts of Victory.

[Enter **DEMAGETUS, ARCASIUS, ALCANDER,** and **SEVERAL OFFICERS,** their Swords drawn as coming from Battle.

DEMAGETUS
A glorious Day, and warmly was it fought:
Nor ever did a Victory more complete
Stoop to the General's Valour –
Some Troops are order'd to secure Phærea;
And with to-morrow's Sun he enters there
To take the Homage of the conquer'd Spartans.

ALCANDER
They say, that Anaxander he has freed
As generously, as he'd ne'er known the Dungeon.

DEMAGETUS
He did, at Prince Aristor's kind Request;
And now, with the high Marks of Conquest crown'd
Is coming to declare to Amalintha
That all her Wishes, and her Fears are ended.

[Turning to go into the Tent, he sees the **BODIES**.

They are, indeed; for ever, ever ended.
Oh! turn and see where that pale Beauty lies,
And faithful, dead Aristor, bleeding by her!

ALCANDER
O sudden Horror! where's our Conquest now,
Our lofty Boasts, and brave expected Triumphs?
Lie there, my Sword, beneath my Leader's Feet;

[Lays his sword at **ARISTOR'S** Feet.

For under him I fought, and now weep for him.

DEMAGETUS
We'll all join to encrease the mournful Shower.
A Soldier for a Soldier's Fall may weep,
And shed these Drops without unmanly Weakness.

[A Sound of Trumpets.

But hark! the Gen'ral, how shall we receive him?
Awhile we'll with our Bodies shade this Prospect,
And tell him by our Looks, some Grief attends him;

Lest all his Fortitude shou'd not support
A Change so sudden in his wretched Fortune.
Nor can we learn from whence this Loss proceeds.

PHILA
Yes, that you may from me: Life yet remains,
And will admit of the too dire Relation.

DEMAGETUS
Then gently bear her hence, and hear it from her.

[They lead off **PHILA**.

That when the Sorrow, which at first must bar
All cold Enquiries, shall awhile be past,
The Gen'ral may be told to what he owes it.
But see! he enters; be we Sad and Silent:
For Oh! too soon this fading Joy must vanish.

[They stand all together before the **BODIES**.

[A FLOURISH of Drums and Trumpets, with Shouts of Joy.

[Enter several **OFFICERS** and **SOLDIERS**, the **SHEPHERDS** and **SHEPHERDESSES** strewing flowers, follow'd by **ARISTOMENES**, his Sword drawn in his Hand, and a Wreath of Victory on his Head.

ARISTOMENES
Enough my Friends! enough my Fellow-Soldiers!
And you kind Shepherds, and your gentle Nymphs,
Receive my Thanks for the Perfumes you scatter,
Which yet shall flourish under our Protection.

SHEPHERD &c.
Great Aristomenes! Live long and happy!

OTHERS
Live long and happy, Father of Messenia!

ARISTOMENES
Now to fair Amalintha wou'd I speak
The joyful Tydings of this Day's Atchievements:
Therefore let her be told, we wish her Presence.

[Seeing none move.

Ha! what none stir! perhaps Aristor's with her:
Why let him tell it; from a Lover's mouth,
'Twill bear a Sound more welcome and harmonious.
And sure in Love and Battle none exceeds him,
The last you all can witness; you saw him Fight,
Saw the young Warrior with his Beaver up

Dart like the Bolt of Jove amongst their Ranks,
And scatter 'em like an Oak's far-shooting Splinters.
Will none confirm it? this is envious Silence.

[Walks up and down.

Thou Demagetus, ha! thou'rt all in Tears,
And so are these that make a Wall about thee:
The Cause deliver, Oh! declare it quickly.

DEMAGETUS
Enquire it not, my Lord; too soon 'twill find you.

ARISTOMENES
I must prevent it by my hasty Search.
Reveal it you, or you, since all partake it:
[To **ALCANDER**, &c.
What silent still! —
If yet ye do not speak, ye do not love me;
I find you do not, since ye all are Speechless.
Aristor wou'd have spoke, had he been here.

DEMAGETUS
Aristor's here, but Oh! he cannot speak.
You have it now, my Lord, and must weep with us.

ARISTOMENES
Thy Tongue has warn'd my Eyes to seek the Centre:

[Looks down.

For round this Place I dare not let them stray,
Lest they explain too soon, thy fatal meaning.
Oh! Anaxander, had such Trembling seiz'd me,
When at the Army's Head I met thy Fury;
The poorest of thy Troops had cry'd me Coward.
Why so we're all, there's not a Man that is not;
We all dread something, and can shrink with Terror:
Yet he that comes a Conqu'ror from the Field,
Shall find a vain Applause to crown his Valour,
Tho' fainting thus, and sweating cold with Fear.

[Pauses and leans on an **OFFICER**.

But didst thou say, Aristor cou'd not speak?
Oh! that I live to ask it! not answer to his Father!

DEMAGETUS
Oh! never more!

ARISTOMENES

The Sun will keep his Pace, and Time revolve,
Rough Winters pass, and Springs come smiling on;
But Thou dost talk of Never, Demagetus:
Yet ere Despair prevails, retract that Word
Whose cloudy distance bars the reach of Thought,
Nor let one Ray of Hope e'er dawn beyond it.
Never, Oh never!

DEMAGETUS [To the **OFFICERS**]
This Passion must rise higher, ere it falls.
Divide, and let him know the worst.

ARISTOMENES
Where is my Son? my Grief has pass'd all Bounds,
All dallying Circumstance, and vain Delusion,
And will be told directly where to find him.

DEMAGETUS
Oh! then behold him there!

[They divide. He seeing the **BODIES** stands awhile amaz'd and speechless, drops his Sword, then speaks.

ARISTOMENES
So look'd the World to Pyrrha, and her Mate;
So gloomy, waste, so destitute of Comfort,
When all Mankind besides lay drown'd in Ruin.
Oh! thou wert well inform'd, my evil Genius;
And the complaining Rocks mourn'd not in vain:
For here my Blood, my dearest Blood I pay
For this poor Wreath, and Fame that withers like it;

[Tears the Wreath, and throws himself upon his **SON**.

The Ground, that bore it, take the slighted Toy,
Whilst thus I throw me on his breathless Body,
And groan away my Life on these pale Lips.
Oh! O', O', O',–
Thus did I clasp him, ere the Battle join'd,
When Fate, which then had Doom'd him, mock'd my Arms,
Nor in their folds wou'd let me feel my Son.
Oh! that his Voice (tho' low as then it seem'd)
Cou'd reach me now!—But the fond Wish is vain,
And all but this too weak to ease my Pain.

[He takes the Sword that lay at **ARISTOR'S** Feet, and goes to fall upon it, **DEMAGETUS** takes hold of it.

DEMAGETUS
Oh! hold, my Lord; nor stab at once your Army.

[All the **OFFICERS** and **SOLDIERS** kneel, **ALCANDER** speaks.

ALCANDER
We're all your Sons; and if you strike, my Lord,
The Spartans may come back, and take our Bodies;
For when yours goes, our Spirits shall attend it.

[They all prepare to fall on their Swords.

ARISTOMENES
Wou'd you then have me live, when thus unbowell'd,
Without the Charms of my Aristor's presence,
Without his Arm to second me in Fight,
And in still Peace his Voice to make it perfect?

[He rises in a Passion and comes forward on the Stage.

Yea, I will live, ye Sov'reign Pow'rs, I will:
You've put my Virtue to its utmost Proof;
Yet thus chastis'd, I own superior Natures,
And all your fixt Decrees this Sword shall further,
'TIll Rhodes is rescu'd, and my Task completed.
Who knows, but that the Way to your Elysium
Is Fortitude in Ills, and brave Submission;
Since Heroes whom your Oracles distinguish,
Are often here amidst their Greatness wretched?
But yet my Heart! my lov'd, my lost Aristor!

DEMAGETUS
Let me succeed him in his active Duty,
And join with all the Earth to bring you Comfort.

ARISTOMENES
Comfort on Earth! Oh! 'tis not to be found.
My Demagetus, thou hast far to travel;
The Bloom of Youth sits graceful on thy Brow,
And bids thee look for Days of might Pleasures,
For prosp'rous Wars, and the soft Smiles of Beauty,
For generous Sons, that may reflect thy Form,
And give thee Hopes, as I had, of their succour.

DEMAGETUS
With these indeed my Thoughts have still been flatter'd.

ARISTOMENES
Then let me draw this flatt'ring Veil aside,
And bid thee here, here in this Face behold,
How biting Cares have done the work of Age,
And in my best of Strength mark'd me a Dotard.
Defeated Armies, slaughter'd Friends are here;
Disgraceful Bonds, and Cities laid in Ashes:

And if thou find'st, that Life will yet endure it,
Since what I here have lost—
So bow'd, so waining shalt thou see this Carcass,
That scarce thou wilt recall what once it was.
Then be instructed Thou, and All that hear me,
Not to expect the compass of soft Wishes,
Or constant Joys, which fly the fond Possessor.
Since Man, by swift returns of Good and Ill,
In all the Course of Life's uncertain still;
By Fortune favour'd now, and now opprest,
And not, 'till Death, secure of Fame, or Rest.

Anne Kingsmill Finch – A Short Biography

Anne Kingsmill was born in April 1661 (an exact date is not known) in Sydmonton, Hampshire. Her parents; Sir William Kingsmill and Anne Haslewood were both from rich and powerful families. Anne was the youngest of three children. When she was only five months her father died but his will stipulated that his daughters receive the same financial support as their brother for education. An unusually enlightened view for the times.

Her mother remarried in 1662, to Sir Thomas Ogle, and later bore Anne's half-sister, Dorothy Ogle, but sadly in 1664 her mother then died. Her will gave control of her estate to her second husband. This was successfully challenged in a Court of Chancery by Anne's uncle, William Haslewood. Subsequently, Anne and her sister Bridget lived with their grandmother, Lady Kingsmill, in Charing Cross, London, while their brother lived with his uncle, William Haslewood.

In 1670, Lady Kingsmill filed her own Court of Chancery suit, requiring a share in the educational and support monies for Anne and Bridget. The court split custody and financial support between Haslewood and Lady Kingsmill. When Lady Kingsmill died in 1672, Anne and Bridget rejoined their brother to be raised by Haslewood.

The sisters received a comprehensive and progressive education, something that was uncommon for females at the time, and Anne learned about Greek and Roman mythology, the Bible, French and Italian languages, history, poetry, and drama.

In 1682, Anne was sent to St James's Palace to become a maid of honour to Mary of Modena (wife of James, Duke of York, later King James II).

Anne's interest in poetry began at the palace, and she started writing her own verse. Her friends included Sarah Churchill and Anne Killigrew, two other maids of honour with poetic interests. However, when Anne witnessed the derision that greeted Killigrew's poetic efforts (a pursuit not considered suitable for women), she decided to keep her own writing attempts to herself and her close friends. This view was to remain with her until much later in life.

While residing at court, Anne met Colonel Heneage Finch. A courtier as well as a soldier, Finch had been appointed Groom of the Bedchamber to James, Duke of York, in 1683. His family had strong Royalist connections, as well as a pronounced loyalty to the Stuart dynasty. Finch fell in love with Anne who at first resisted but Finch proved a persistent and successful suitor.

The couple married on 15th May 1684 and Anne resigned her court position. Her husband retained his own appointment and would also serve in various government positions. The couple were determined to remain involved in court life.

The marriage was enduring and happy, in part due to the equality in their partnership. Her poetic skills blossomed as she expressed her love for her husband and the positive effects of his support on her artistic development.

Their life was rather sedate but when James II took the throne Heneage became more involved in public affairs. The couple were very loyal to the king in what turned out to be a brief reign. James II was deposed in 1688 during the "Bloodless Revolution" when William of Orange was offered the English crown. When the new monarchs, William and Mary, both Protestants, assumed the throne, oaths of allegiance were required from both the public and the clergy. The Finches refused to take the oath and remained loyal to the Catholic Stuart court. This invited trouble. Heneage lost his government position, his income and retreated from public life. The Finches were forced to live with friends in London where they faced harassment, fines and the threat of imprisonment.

In April 1690, Heneage was arrested and charged with Jacobitism. Heneage and Anne would remain separated from April until November of that year. This caused the couple a great deal of emotional turmoil. Anne often fell ill to bouts of depression, something that afflicted her for most of her adult life. Her work was noticeably less playful than her earlier poems.

After Finch was released and his case dismissed, his nephew Charles Finch, the fourth Earl of Winchelsea, invited them to move into the family estate at Eastwell Park, Kent. The Finches took up residence in late 1690 and found peace and security. They would reside there for the next 25 years.

For Anne the estate provided fertile ground for her literary efforts which were encouraged by both Charles and Heneage. Her husband's support was also practical. He collected a portfolio of her 56 poems, writing them out by hand and made small changes. One significant change involved her pen name, which he changed from "Areta" to "Ardelia".

King William died in 1702, and his death was followed by the succession of Queen Anne, the daughter of James II (who had died the previous year). With these developments, the Finches felt ready to embrace a more public lifestyle. Finch ran for parliament three times (in 1701, 1705, and 1710), but was never elected. Still, they now felt ready to leave the country and move to London.

In London, Anne was encouraged to publish her poetry. In 1701 she published "The Spleen" anonymously. This well-received reflection on depression would prove to be her most popular poem.

Anne also acquired some influential friends, including Jonathan Swift and Alexander Pope, who encouraged her to write and publish much more openly. She was reluctant, as she felt the climate still remained oppressive for women. When she published 'Miscellany Poems, on Several Occasions' in 1713, the cover page of the first printing stated that the work was "Written by a Lady." On subsequent printings, she received credit as Anne, Countess of Winchilsea.

Anne became Countess of Winchilsea upon the sudden and unexpected death of the childless Charles Finch on 4th August 1712. However, the titles came with a cost. They had to assume and discharge Charles Finch's financial and legal burdens. This was eventually settled in the Finches' favour, after seven years of further emotional strain, in 1720.

They also faced renewed strains from court politics. When Queen Anne died in 1714, she was succeeded by George I. Subsequently, a Whig government, hostile to the Jacobite cause, came to power. The Jacobite rebellion of 1715, further aggravated the political situation. They were now concerned for their safety.

These and other worries combined started to take a toll on Anne's health, which began to deteriorate. In 1715 she became seriously ill. Her later poems spoke of this. In particular, 'A Suplication for the Joys of Heaven' and 'A Contemplation' expressed her concerns about her life, political and spiritual beliefs.

Anne Kingsmill-Finch died on August 5th 1720 in Westminster, London. Her body was returned to Eastwell for burial, according to her previously stated wishes.

In her obituary her husband praised her talents as a writer and her virtues as an individual. A portion of it read, "To draw her Ladyship's just Character, requires a masterly Pen like her own (She being a fine Writer, and an excellent Poet); we shall only presume to say, she was the most faithful Servant to her Royall Mistresse, the best Wife to her Noble Lord, and in every other Relation, publick and private, so illustrious an Example of such extraordinary Endowments, both of Body and Mind, that the Court of England never bred a more accomplished Lady, nor the Church of England a better Christian."

Anne Kingsmill Finch – A Concise Bibliography

Upon the Death of King James the Second (1701)
The Tunbridge Prodigy (1706)
The Spleen, A Pindarique Ode. By a Lady (1709)
Free-thinkers: A Poem in Dialogue (1711)
Miscellany Poems, on Several Occasions. Written by a Lady (1713)

Editions and Collections
The Poems of Anne Countess of Winchilsea, edited by Myra Reynolds (1903)
Selected Poems of Anne Finch, Countess of Winchilsea (1906)
Poems, by Anne, Countess of Winchilsea, compiled by John Middleton Murry (1928)

www.ingramcontent.com/pod-product-compliance
Lightning Source LLC
Chambersburg PA
CBHW051702040426
42446CB00009B/1258